*Sno*

*& Flood*
**on**
# EXMOOR

Martin Hesp

EXMOOR PRESS

ISBN 0 900131 71 3

**British Library Cataloguing-in-publication Data**

A CIP catalogue record for this book is available from the British Library.

EXMOOR PRESS
Dulverton, Somerset

*Trade sales enquires:*
Halsgrove
Halsgrove House
Lower Moor Way
Tiverton, EX16 6SS
Tel: 01884 243242
Fax: 01884 243325

Printed and bound in Great Britain by WBC Ltd, Bridgend

# CONTENTS

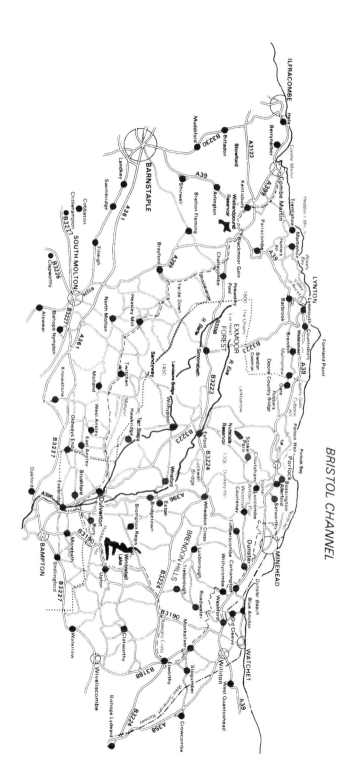

# INTRODUCTION

When the voice on the radio warns of gales for areas Lundy-Fastnet-Shannon-Irish Sea you will find the more experienced residents of remote parts of the Westcountry putting another log on the fire and battening down the hatches. For what brews itself into a rage along these sea areas of the Western Approaches must, within an hour or two, certainly hit our peninsula with all the violence wind and the weather can muster.

And few places take the brunt of the weather more fully than the heights of Exmoor – a range of hills well and truly in the meteorological firing line thanks to a blustery mixture of altitude and close proximity to the sea.

This book examines some of the more extreme weather conditions which have hit the greater Exmoor region over the centuries – occurrences which have in some cases caused tragic deaths as well as extreme hardship and extensive damage to buildings and property.

What often comes as a result of nature throwing her worst at man, is great courage and fortitude, and many of the stories in this book illustrate feats of selfless bravery carried out by ordinary people caught up in the maelstrom of blizzard and gale. For a good deal of the information here in the author and publishers are enormously indebted to the late Jack Hurley, the well known editor of the *West Somerset Free Press*, who in 1975 published the original *Snow and Storm on Exmoor*. Indeed Jack's entertaining and informative book creates much of the core of this volume, but I have added extensive notes from my father Peter Hesp's files which cover nearly fortyyears of his news-reporting in the area for the *Somerset County Gazette*.

Elsewhere I have interviewed survivors of some of the more dramatic events and would like to extend my thanks to them for patiently relaying to me details of their extraordinary adventures brought about by the vagaries and violence of Exmoor's erratic weather...

## *From the Sublime to the Ridiculous*

As its title suggests, this book is about the great storms and blizzards suffered by the region over the ages, and yet we begin by noting that the high hills of Exmoor once enjoyed an altogether warmer, gentler climate. More Dordogne the Dunkery, you might say. Pollen tests carried out in the peat on the high moor by scientists from Cambridge University revealed an altogether different flora was to be found here 1000 to 2000 years BC. This presumably made it possible for the Bronze Age folk to lead more-or-less comfortable lives on what nowadays can be very draughty hilltops – which was just as well, as the thick vegetation of the valleys and vales would have made them just about impenetrable to a people armed with not much more than a flint or bronze axe.

Of course, the Ice Age had scraped at Exmoor's shores many millennia before that, but as there was no-one recording either anecdote or meteorology back in those days, let's begin with some firm evidence of storm and strife in the hills...

The first mention I can find in the Somerset Record Office of adverse weather on Exmoor is, alas, a tragic one. It comes from a brief minute in the Porlock Tithing of 30 December, 1320, and it concerns a family who had just had their Christmas spoiled in a macabre and horrible way. The inquest at Porlock heard how one Nicholas de Harewode, of Lucott, Stoke Pero, set out into the snow on Christmas Eve to search for his daughter Eghelina de Harewode whom he knew to be walking the long route home from 'Molton' in Devon. Which of the two Moltons, the minutes of the inquest fail to record, but whether it was North or South it was a serious walk to be undertaken by anyone on a summer's day, let alone in the mid-winter conditions poor Eghelina found herself struggling through. The inquest handed down its icy verdict: 'At Bellbrooke night and snow overcame her and buried her body – whereby she died of misadventure.'

The next we hear of snow making an appearance in public records is in the Selworthy Church Register for 1744. The copperplate insertion is as brief as it is chilly: 'Richard Gould was buried November 21st. Died in snow on Porlock Hills, November 17th.'

But snow of course, isn't the only weapon in the armoury of foul weather. Indeed great rains have accounted for many more human souls than Exmoor's infamous giant drifts. Take for instance the 'Second Deluge' as it was known at the time, the terrible floods of 1607 which 'caused great loss of life and property in the county of Somersetshire.'

So recorded an excellently written contemporary piece of journalism entitled 'A True Report of Certain Wonderful Overflowings of Waters in Somersetshire, Norfolk and Other Parts of England'.

According to the author the county of Somerset was hit far worse than any other during this once-in-a-millennium deluge which, 'Destroyed many thousands of men, women and children, overthrowing and bearing downe whole townes and villages and drowning infinite numbers of sheepe and other cattle.

'Bankes were eaten through and ruptured waters into Somersetshire. The "daunger" this terrible tempest brought w'it wrought much fear in the hearts of all that stood within reach of it.

'Men that were going to their labours were compelled (seeing so dreadful an enemy approaching) to flye backe to their houses, yet before they could enter, death stood at the dores ready to receive them.'

Indeed there is an account in the book of an unfortunate Somerset father who attempted to save his seven children from the flood – but they were all swept from the thatched roof of the small cottage – six of them perishing and one, the youngest, being washed up half-a-mile away in its buoyant crib.

The poetic writer goes on: 'Oxen in great numbers were caryed away with the stream, and looked like so many Whales in ye Sea...

'Nay, which is more strange, conies (rabbits) in great numbers being driven out of their borroughs by the tyde, were seen to sit for safety on the backs of sheepe as they swam up and downe and at last were drowned with them.'

And they say global warming is making a mess of the weather nowadays!

But if you're not convinced by all this meteorological mayhem happening in days of yore, then what about this from the parish clerk of the Somerset village of Ubley in 1703:

'It pleased God to afflict us with such a tempest we were afraid to lie in our beds, we were afraid to sit by the fire, afraid to abide in our households and afraid to go forth into the field...'

He leaves us with a firm impression that he was more than a little nervous. Call him lily-livered if you will, but why not be afraid? On that dreadful night of 26 November he tells us that church towers were torn down, entire roofs were blown off buildings and even stone walls were thrown asunder.

'It blew such a wind it seemed likely to threaten to blow the land into the sea and lift the sea into the land.

'It is a night such to be remembered of all the peoples in England in their generation.'

Even modern TV weathermen have been known to get these major meteorological events wrong, but atmospheric conditions are strange and moody things and if they're under the control of some Almighty being one thing only is for sure: He might know where and when and how violent the storm will be, but we mere mortals can only guess. Which makes it in a way all the more ironic that Westcountry churches have a long history of falling victim to these vigorous acts of God. At Porlock, St Dubricius once had a spire, but this was blown off in a gale sometime around the year 1700 – perhaps in 1703 in the great storm described by the Clerk of

Ubley. But whenever the exact date legend has it that the spire was blown all the way to Culbone where it sits pertly on the top of England's smallest complete church to this day. And if you study Culbone Church, there is indeed something odd about the spire which looks for all the world as if it might have been borrowed from somewhere else.

Some two decades later the good people of Crowcombe, tucked under the Quantock Hills just outside the Exmoor National Park, may have been forgiven for thinking that God had taken against them. In 1725 their splendid red sandstone church also boasted a fine spire until the night a violent lightning bolt sent it crashing to the ground. The top of this architectural relic was saved from destruction and can still be seen standing in the graveyard as an age-old reminder that freak weather is not just a modern day phenomenon.

# 1 THE LATE 1800s

*Lifeboat to the rescue*

The value of human life had become slightly more cherished by the end of the nineteenth century and the sad deaths of those lost in severe weather began to warrant more than just a one line note in a parish register. Perhaps this hypothesis is ill-founded and it was simply a case that more people were inclined to record events on paper, but nevertheless human life was deemed important enough to see the setting up of organised rescue services.

It was back in 1824 that Sir William Hillary helped to inaugurate the National Institution for the Preservation of Life from Shipwreck, later to become the RNLI. This excellent service became represented locally at Watchet in 1875. That was when the ancient port took delivery of the 33 -foot, rowing, sailing and self-righting lifeboat named *Joseph Somes*.

With a lifeboat house on The Esplanade just inland of the harbour, it can be imagined that rescues could often be laborious affairs thanks to the area's dubious honour of having the second highest tidefall in the world. In other words, low water launches meant the crew employing the help of at least eight heavy horses to drag the boat on its heavy carriage across the harbour and out across the rough and rocky foreshore.

April 1878 saw one such launch when a terrific north easterly was blasting down the Bristol Channel blowing anything afloat towards the Somerset and North Devon shore. The *Rose*, a Gloucester trow, was spotted dragging her anchor just two miles from Watchet and orders were given to launch the lifeboat. Being low-water the crew had a herculean struggle on their hands to get their big heavy boat out across the reefs and natural rock pavements which they had to cross the reach the sea. And they were in a hurry because it had been reported that a man had been seen out on the decks of the *Rose*, so they knew lives were at stake.

The bad news is that the *Joseph Somes* reached the scene too late, the trow having smashed aground on the rocks – but the good news was that a team of Coastguards was on the spot and able to save the lives of those aboard. However, it turned out to be most fortuitous that the lifeboat was now at sea: by now the sloop *Olive Branch* of Cardiff was suffering the same fate as the *Rose* and, through the skilful efforts of the lifeboat crew and her stand-in skipper Henry Press, the merchantman's captain and crew were saved. Alas the great storm hammered the sloop onto the rocks within a stone's throw of the rapidly disintegrating trow.

### *Deep Freeze, Hurricane and Blizzard All In One*

So much for violent gales, but just three years later England, and the Exmoor region, was to suffer one of the worst blizzards for more than a century when hurricane winds were lethally accompanied by sub-zero temperatures as well as great falls of snow.

Across the country and at sea, many hundreds of men, women and children lost their lives in the extreme weather conditions of 18 January, 1881. Some were found frozen to death – still standing where they'd been making their way to work. Entire families belonging to the poorer classes died in wretched tenements unable to keep warm enough to sustain life in the terrible freeze. A man, his wife and their three children froze to death in the snow just outside Warminster. The woman was in the final stages of her pregnancy.

Teams of horses were dug out of deep drifts, frozen dead in their shafts. Shepherds were found sitting upright with their hands above their heads in some vain attempt to keep off the snow. They had perished with their sheep. A farmer from near Chard in South Somerset was extracted from a drift and it took 12 healthy men five hours to haul his corpse the one mile back to town. In the big freeze, graves were difficult to dig so the poor chap was kept on ice, as it were, for eight days. This caused a rumour to circulate in the area that he had come back to life again – one taken so seriously that a local doctor took it upon himself to inspect the body just to make sure.

Across Europe this mini Ice Age caused havoc in its chilly, gale-blown grip. For the only time on record the Sound of Copenhagen was frozen over allowing people to cross from Denmark to Sweden on foot.

Closer to home Britain's single worst disaster in that freezing blast from the Arctic occurred at Great Yarmouth where seven vessels were blown ashore with the loss of almost 100 lives – including six of the lifeboat crew.

The same gale sank 100 barges in the River Thames killing many boatmen. Indeed few would have recognised England's great river which by now was full of 'ice-boulders' causing havoc and flooding before the waters froze over completely. On 17 January, the day before the storm, the temperature in London was recorded as minus 18 degrees Fahrenheit.

For those in good health or with the wherewithal to survive these freak conditions, the experience could prove to be a novelty. At Twickenham they were enjoying sheep-roasting parties on the frozen river while in Somerset one man let his imagination and his entrepreneurism run wild. Thomas Buller's brilliant, if eccentric idea for an ice palace was realised as a way of raising money for the poor, the cold and the hungry of Wellington, and many hundreds of people travelled to see this unique marvel once it was built. One room in the palace was 40 feet long and 27 wide and the ice-house, perhaps unique in the history of this country, could accommodate 450 people, each paying four old pence for admission. It took 50 men three days to build and inside a gas supply was laid on so that hot beverages could be served.

Nearly every railway in the Westcountry came to a standstill thanks to the thick snow and the lines around Exmoor were no exception. Three trains and seven engines were snowed up for days and the Taunton to Minehead branch line was closed for a week because cuttings were blocked by drifts up to 30 feet deep. After five days the Devon and Somerset line was cleared as far as Molland, but at that point the labourers were sent home being on the brink of physical collapse.

At Dulverton able-bodied men showed heart-warming solidarity with less fortunate citizens by shovelling a path clear so that Poor Law relieving officer Mr Stone could get around to pay a shilling each to people dependent on parish relief.

But perhaps the single most compelling story of the great storm of 1881 concerns the case of the forgotten sailor. Imagine being knocked about in the Bristol Channel on a Norwegian barque in one of the worst storms in an entire millennium only to find you've been abandoned by all your shipmates! That's exactly what happened to Tallac Oslem, ship's carpenter on the 529 ton *American* which had parted her cable while riding out the storm in Penarth Roads. A tug boat had taken her in tow until, finding they were drifting on a lee shore, the barque's crew were transferred and the tow ropes slipped. Why the carpenter had gone below, history does not reveal, but what is known is that when the poor man re-emerged on deck he found himself alone in one of the most terrible maelstroms over witnessed in the Channel.

In these days of rigid procedures it's hard to imagine a ship's crew calmly abandoning a vessel without checking numbers – but whether they simply forgot poor Tallac in the horror of the moment, or whether he'd done something to make himself horribly unpopular, we'll never know. What is certain is that the carpenter stayed aboard for some time before realising that the barque was doomed to smash onto the rocks of the West Somerset coast. Now he abandoned ship himself taking the ship's tender in a desperate last ditch attempt to save his own life. Perhaps, through the gale and the blizzard, he was able to make out the mud beyond the surf at Blue Anchor and thought he'd stand more of a chance trying to land there. After all, mud is a lot softer than rock. Anyway, it was to Blue Anchor that this desperate seafarer managed to guide his cockleshell of a boat and he must have had a soft landing of it because the next we hear of him is at the railway station.

Maybe it was the only illumination he could see along the dark coast on this most terrible of nights, but whatever caused him to go there it was nearly his undoing. The problem was that he chose the house of station-master William Crang, an individual remarkable for being of a particularly nervous disposition, not to mention quite deaf. The highly strung Crang always kept a loaded revolver close to him for fear of intruders, and the half-drowned carpenter covered in slimy Blue Anchor mud must have cut a frightening figure in the middle of the night. The station-master held the gun to Oslem's head which undoubtedly caused him to achieve some pretty fast and loud talking as, in the end, he avoided the undeserved death of a bullet in the brain.

Not far off that same night, more adventure was occurring in the tempest. West, beyond the *American* (which was finally hurled ashore at Warren Point, near Minehead) the barque *Tarsus* was being smashed onto the razor-like rocks of Hurlestone Point at the edge of Porlock Bay. Here again the human struggle for survival cheated death as the ten-man crew lashed themselves to her decks before being able to escape across the rocks as the tide receded.

West again and we come to the pilot boat *Cambria*, stripped of her canvas, leaving John Dibden and John Union to drift helplessly through that terrible night. They must have been two very nervous men indeed that awful dawn when the first light revealed that they were closing in on Lynmouth's rockbound coast. Believing they stood more of a chance making a run for it Union and Dibden took to the cutter's punt and made for shore at a point between two enormous rocks at Ridiball. As onlookers predicted the punt was soon swamped and it was a miracle that Dibden was able to save himself, while his shipmate was twice swept back into the raging sea. He would doubtless have drowned if the courageous Philip Burgess, master of the *Nautilus*, of Lynmouth, had not been there. Three times in twelve months Burgess had saved the lives of drowning men, and he was not about to let his reputation down. He dived into the boiling surf and managed to rescue John Union just minutes before their boat *Cambria* was dashed to pieces on that very shore.

Later as the toll of the storm of the century was tallied, the *West Somerset Free Press* was relieved to report the following: 'It is a matter for congratulation that although so many lives were lost, both on land and sea, in this fearful storm, yet in the Exmoor district, so far as we have heard, there has not been a single case of death, either through the violence of the storm or through exposure.'

## *A Decade Later Snows Return*

The same newspaper was reporting more tragic winter news ten years later when an Exmoor man met his end in the blizzard of 1891. He was Amos Cann of Smallacombe, near Exford, and his undoing was his concern for his aged father. Young Amos had gone into Porlock on the morning of 9 March to attend to some business and it was at 8.00 that evening when he made the tragic decision to brave the weather and return home. A Porlock friend, Edwin Arnold, begged him to stay the night because of the heavy snow but Amos knew his father, who suffered from rheumatism, would never be able to cope with the sheep.

Exmoor's giant drifts did not give up their dead until seventeen days later when Cann's perfectly preserved body was dug out of deep snow near the hunting gate at Alderman's Barrow – about a mile from his home. For more than two weeks search parties had been out on the moor and they were aided by Fenwick Bissett, Master of the Devon and Somerset Staghounds, who allowed the pack to be used in the hunt.

It was conjectured that Amos Cann had been trying to find the gate when, climbing the hedge, he had fallen backwards and been too exhausted to get up.

There's a painful sub-plot to this tragic tale in which Police Superintendent Ross of Wiveliscombe had reached Brompton Regis on his way to investigate the case of the missing Amos Cann, when his horse bolted, threw him, and kicked him in the head. The policeman was patched up at the inn, but was unable to continue onto Exmoor.

Elsewhere on Exmoor the blizzard was causing havoc. Farmers digging sheep out of drifts were finding that only half their animals had survived. With the road between Dulverton and Exford being impassable no doctor was able to visit the latter village for more than two weeks.

At Dulverton the Poor Law guardians were called to an emergency meeting but only two of their number managed to get there. At least three were required to make a quorum and it was only after half-an-hour that C.H. Glass was spied making his way through the snow. It was then proposed and seconded that latecomers should be fined the price of dinner for the other guardians – a decision Mr Glass did not happily second!

Once they had got down to the serious business in hand they approved of the sum of £20. 3s. 6d. being distributed among 190 paupers in the district and decided to purchase, among articles of clothing for the Workhouse inmates, woman's stays at 2s. 6d. a pair.

The local Highway Boards faced a good deal of criticism during and after the 1891 blizzard because they had been so reluctant to spend money on snow clearance. Having occurred in March the argument was that Nature would soon clear up after herself. It turned out she was reluctant to do so and eventually Dulverton Board shelled out £42. 10s. 9., Williton Board £10 less, while Dunster Board refused to spend any money at all. In the end they had to give in but even then stipulated that parish waywardens could not embark upon the clearance until the following Monday and that no such work should be carried out thereafter.

And we modern motorists bemoan our fate when stuck in a traffic jam today....

Once again, this blizzard was responsible for the wholesale stoppage of train services across the region. Perhaps the most remarkable incident was the journey of the G.W.R 'Zulu' train from London to Penzance which took four days to reach Cornwall. Stuck in drifts near the village of Brent the passengers witnessed the more unattractive side of human nature which can occasionally rear its ugly head in an hour of need. The locals immediately doubled the price of everything when they realised there was a train-load of desperate people with nowhere else to go. Indeed, had the driver not kept his engine going throughout the ordeal some passengers might have frozen to death. They were even left unimpressed by the actions of the local clergyman who didn't bother turning up to see if anything could be done to help the stricken travellers until the day of the train's release!

## Selfless Courage at Sea

We must return to Watchet and its lifeboat if we wish to remind ourselves that, for every mean-spirited action there were plenty of examples of self-less and heroic deeds towards the stormy end of that century. This time it was the turn of the new lifeboat, the *W.H.G. Kingston*, to put to sea in a terrible gale during November of 1899.

A Minehead herring fishing boat – the *Rosalie* – was spotted in the dark just west of the town's harbour and even through the din of the huge waves, men's cries could be heard shouting for help. In fact the two-man crew were exhausted with long exposure to the intense cold and had been reduced to a state where they were unable to handle their small vessel. The lifeboat was launched, once again with great difficulty as the tide had only reached the mouth of the harbour. But no sooner was she afloat than the coxswain began to realise that his crew would stand no chance against the wind and tide. The *W.H.G. Kingston* was swept up-channel away from the vessel in distress.

Among the onlookers huddled on the quayside was *West Somerset Free Press* reporter Willie Lee (for many years Honorary Secretary to the lifeboat) and he filed the following report:

An hour passes with no sign of the lifeboat. Meanwhile the despairing cries of the men in jeopardy continue. A suggestion is made that a smaller and lighter boat might be able to reach the fishing boat whereas the heavy lifeboat has failed. Captain's Escott, Wedlake, Davis and A.&S. Nicholas are in consultation. The sea has moderated slightly and it is thought that if action is to be taken it must be now or never. Captain Davis gets his small boat with a staff of oars etc., and is immediately joined by the other four Master Mariners. Captain Escott takes charge and amid tumultuous cheering the brave fellows are off. For a moment the elements seem determined to check them – an enormous wave striking the piles as the boat's nose comes out into the harbour mouth, but they safely emerge through the broken water and pull away. Being low in the water the wind has not got much hold on the boat and she goes through the water at a rate which gladdens the heart of the spectators. In a minute or two she is lost to sight – a second or so later she reappears, a black object under the light of the moon's rays, and then disappears. It seems but a minute or two when she is seen returning, and disappointment is writ large as it is generally conjectured that she has failed in her object. 'She's got 'em' shouts a stentorian voice from the rail of the breakwater, and amid a torrent of cheering from hundreds of throats, the boat returns to the harbour with the two fishermen – John Bryant and George Wills. They are landed at the breakwater amid a scene of tremendous enthusiasm and are quickly borne off to Mrs Lee's Refreshment Rooms where restoratives and everything necessary are found for the men. Bryant quickly recovers, but Wills is not so fortunate and it takes a good deal of work on the part of several willing helpers to restore animation to his body and limbs which are almost ice-cold.

Back at sea the disappointed crew of the lifeboat anchored and waited until conditions favoured their return. They were rewarded in their endeavours by being told soon after that the Watchet station was to close while a new one was to be opened at Minehead. Meanwhile the Institute awarded Captain Escott with a pair of binoculars while Captains A. and S. Nicholas, A. Wedlake and J. Davis each received an aneroid barometer.

Naturally the high spirited men of Watchet were appalled when the RNLI later decided to remove their boat because of a replacement which was now in service at Minehead, and put up such a good fight to save the station that there was a reprieve which lasted until the Second World War.

# 2  OVERLAND HEROES

On a black stormy night in January 1899 a single telegram, which arrived in the tiny North Devon harbour village of Lynmouth, was to result in a maritime rescue of such epic proportions that 100 years later the world's media turned out to record the centenary re-enactment of one of the most famous lifeboat rescues ever staged and television pictures and newspaper images of the event were relayed around the planet.

Reporting the re-enactment for the *Western Morning News* I watched as sleet obliterated Exmoor's coastal hill-tops and high winds sent white horses scurrying across the grey waters of the Bristol Channel. The scene down on Lynmouth's Esplanade could have been authentic as enormous cart horses were attached to a 40-foot trailer carrying a period lifeboat, in preparation for the long haul to Porlock. But in the dark light of dawn, the scenario was strangely surreal as the torrential rain dripped down onto the gathered crowds from the dishes of several TV satellite communication trucks. Technicians at work in their glowing interiors linked North Devon with the world as camera crews milled about among the hundreds of onlookers and helpers, many of whom were in period dress.

So why stage a centenary re-enactment of a lifeboat rescue and why the international interest? The answer is simple enough – to this day the people of Lynmouth and its sister village of Lynton are rightly proud of the extraordinary courage and determination shown by their forefathers who performed the remarkable feat generally known as the 'Overland Haul'. A feat which Jack Hurley was later to describe as, 'Exmoor's contribution to a national roll of notable deeds.'

It was on Thursday 12 January 1899, that a nor-westerly gale was increasing to almost hurricane strength as it bore down upon Exmoor's rugged coastline. Not a good place to be at sea in such conditions and an appalling berth if your vessel was equipped only with sail. Such was the situation in Porlock Bay where a big, full-rigged iron ship was dragging her anchors and in trouble. By late afternoon the master of the *Forrest*

*Hall* ordered the distress rockets to be launched and from that moment the wheels of one of Britain's most remarkable maritime rescues slowly began to turn – though the word maritime might be a bit of a misnomer because much of the desperate deed was accomplished on land.

Porlock Bay lay between areas covered by two lifeboats and early that fateful evening the crew at Watchet were telegraphing their colleagues up and down the coast that they were unable to launch because of sea and tide conditions. They sent this missive to Lynmouth at 7.30pm but, because of the vagaries of the archaic communications system, the telegram was not received until 10.30pm, by which time the historic journey was well underway. There was some irony in this because an overland launch from Watchet to Porlock would have been more easily accomplished thanks to flatter, easier, roads – but then, we wouldn't have such an heroic tale to tell.

We can pick up on the beginning of the story by listening, a century later, to bowler-hatted local businessman John Pedder, telling numerous TV camera crews how it all started. Dressed for the re-enactment as his own grandfather, Mr Pedder was explaining how his relation became very much part of the extraordinary rescue:

'He had the post office at Lynmouth and he received the telegram by morse from Porlock to alert the lifeboat. He took it down to the lifeboat house where Jack Crocombe, who was the coxswain, was waiting along with some of the others because it was a very rough sea – and sailors always congregate when conditions are bad.

'The coxswain made the decision to launch at Porlock and the maroon went up,' said Mr Pedder. 'It was a north-west gale and there was no other place which they could have possibly launched in those conditions.'

What is particularly remarkable about the decision to take their boat *Louisa* overland was that the Lynmouth crew had no details whatsoever about the state-of-play concerning the beleaguered *Forrest Hall*.

'That was the depth of the sense of duty held by these men,' said Mr Pedder. 'The rules at the time stated you should haul the lifeboat to a place where it could be safely put to sea – if one were available. These skilful seamen knew there was a chance Porlock Weir would offer just such shelter.'

Mr Pedder's grandfather decided to go along to survey the situation in his official capacity as the local Lloyds Register agent: not only did he travel overland to Porlock, but actually sailed with the crew to help in the rescue.

Recounting the event as it was reported in the *West Somerset Free Press*, writer Jack Hurley later summed up this seemingly crazy rescue attempt in the following terms:

'Under cool examination – for which there was then no time – the idea would seem preposterous. One could marshal a dozen objections to it.

'A wild night's journey over one of the worst roads in the country, rising to almost 1400 feet. A terrific ascent (Countisbury) at the beginning, a perilous drop (Porlock) at the end. Pitch darkness relieved only by flickering lanterns which would frequently blow out. A coast road that was then little more than a rough lane. Places where the lifeboat carriage would jam, where banks and gateposts would have to be knocked down; one section so narrow that the boat would have to be taken off the carriage and the carriage transferred to moorland.

'No, the idea was too fantastic to entertain. Yet here are the crew and launchers translating it into action, their only thought that lives are in danger on the sea...'

Just about everyone in Lynton and Lynmouth turned out to see the epic start, so that there were plenty of willing hands to give a shove as the boat on its carriage, drawn by 20 horses, began the long ascent of Countisbury Hill. Those first two miles broke the heart of many of the helpers. When, at the top of the hill, a lynch-pin broke and the boat carriage lost a wheel, many of the townsfolk turned back – soaked through in the driving rain.

About 20 men grimly continued, patiently jacking up the carriage and refixing the wheel while the storm raged and, somewhere in Porlock Bay, a helpless ship drifted towards the rocks.

Meanwhile signalman R. Moor had gone ahead with half-a-dozen men removing obstacles, including a wall near Glenthorne White Gate, to make way for the ponderous load that was to follow. When the lifeboat caught up with them, at Ashton Lane on the 1050 foot contour, the straining, sweating, rain soaked men were in despair. It was impossible for them to widen the whole half mile stretch of lane.

Tom Bevan, who was later to become secretary of the lifeboat, later recalled: 'Jack Crocombe said we had come so far and we were not going to turn back. We had first to take the boat off its carriage and while some were doing that others were digging down gateposts to let the carriage go through to the moors.'

So while one party took the lightened carriage around, the remainder hauled the boat itself through the lane on skids. After a Herculean struggle the boat was eventually able to rejoin its carriage and so the journey resumed at faster pace. The next great obstacle was Porlock Hill with its infamous gradient. After topping Hawkcombe Head at 1400 feet, ropes and wheel drags were attached to the cumbersome load to check the forward impetus. As a final precaution the lifeboat was securely lashed down to prevent it sliding forwards off its carriage and onto the horses.

It was a job well done. The descent went smoothly without incident until they reached the cottages at the bottom. Here they had to knock down a couple of garden walls, much to the indignation of a mob-capped old lady, who objected to being so rudely awakened in the small hours. However, when she heard the mission of the lifeboat, she caught up her shawl and joined in to help.

On went the boat towards Porlock Weir, until a man came running to say that the seafront road was awash and impassable. Nothing could stop these grim, grey faced men at this stage. They hauled their boat over

Mariner's Combe, chopping down a great tree which barred their way, and so came successfully down to the shore at Porlock Weir.

It was now six in the morning and the men were staggering with fatigue, drenched to the skin and both hungry and thirsty. But somewhere out there on the sea in the driving spray the crew of a stricken ship was waiting for their help. Without pause the lifeboatmen put to sea, straining their oars with every faculty alert as the combers threatened to overwhelm their craft.

Their overland journey, unique in the annals of the RNLI, was done and it is easy to forget the rest of the story. For the tough men of Lynmouth however, the work had just begun.

After beating through the storm for an hour and a half they found the *Forrest Hall* drifting towards the lee shore with both anchors down. Her rudder had been lost leaving her quite helpless. As daylight broke the lifeboat made contact with the tug *Jane Joliffe*, and succeeded in taking a line from that vessel down to the stricken ship.

Some of the lifeboatmen boarded the Liverpool-based ship to help haul in the anchors, and then the three vessels set off for the long haul across the wind to Barry in South Wales.

Little is recorded of those weary hours with sail and oar, but it is known that the *Forrest Hall* was well nigh unmanageable in her rudderless condition. The *Free Press* reported:

Fortunately the ship was got to Barry Roads in safe anchorage. When she let go her anchors the lifeboatmen made for Barry where, on their arrival at 5.00 p.m., the dock authorities showed them every kindness, and they were taken by the local agent of the Shipwrecked Mariners Society to the Dolphin Restaurant.

All the men bore traces of their severe buffeting, having had scarcely anything to eat and drink for 24 hours, and some had been aboard the lifeboat since she had left Porlock. They had had an awful experience, towing on the weather side of the ship across the Channel. In their opinion the ship had not hands sufficient or ballast enough to go from Bristol to Liverpool (her intended journey).

The lifeboat left Barry on Saturday morning in tow of the *s.s. Letbury* of London, and arrived safely at Lynmouth at 11.00 a.m.

Whether or not they received a heroes' welcome the newspaper does not recount. But here are a few more of the facts that we do know.

The lifeboatmen who took part in the epic rescue were: John Crocombe (coxswain), G.S. Richards, R. Burgess, W. Richards, R. Ridler, G. Rawle, J. Ward, W. Jarvis, Charles Crick, B. Pennicott, David Crocombe, John Ridler and T. Pugsley.

That night was the first call-out for W. Richards who, as youngest member of the crew, was just 16.

They received awards of £5 each while the launchers collected a total of £27. 5s. 6d. The total cost of the night's service, including awards, hire of horses, and a mason's bill for repairs, was £118. 17s. 9d. Towards it the owners of the *Forrest Hall* contributed £75.

Lastly, it was realised that the distance between the Lynmouth and Watchet boats left an over-large hole in the RNLI service along this dangerous stretch of coast, and one year later a lifeboat was stationed at Minehead. Ironically perhaps, it is the only station of the three to remain in active service.

As for the centenary re-enactment, it passed authentically enough in driving rain throughout the overland journey section.

The boat reached Porlock by mid-afternoon and the sun came out as they were welcomed by thousands of onlookers as well as by camera crews and TV helicopters. Later, in the bars at Porlock Weir, the volunteers who had dragged the boat the 14 miles were agreeing that the original rescuers must have been made of stern stuff indeed.

Watching the Barry and Minehead lifeboats bobbing alarmingly about in steep waves, each of the burly but weary re-enactment crew was of one mind – enough was enough, and none welcomed the idea of setting out in wild seas after such a journey.

*The centenary re-enactment of the Lynmouth lifeboat haul, January 1999.* (Steve Guscott)

*Watchet Harbour after the storm, 1900.* (H.H.Hole)

# 3  A NEW CENTURY BLOWN IN

Woodworm and waves combined to exacerbate one of the most costly storm disasters ever to occur along the West Somerset coast – a destruction which caused hardened sailors watching helplessly from the shore, to break down in tears of grief as most of Watchet's fleet of wooden ships were smashed to matchwood.

Thursday 27 December saw a sou'wester blowing fiercely up the Channel which, by nightfall, had turned threateningly into a raging gale howling directly in from the west.  The threat came, as it almost always does in the Bristol Channel, when wind and incoming tide combined to create the dreaded phenomenon known as a surge.  Tide levels and waves can both be higher in these surges which to this day are feared by coastal engineers for their potential to flood.

But in 1900 the authorities at Watchet had a good deal more to worry about than the temporary inconvenience of flooding – the very fabric of the harbour was at stake.  Woodworm had been eating at the timber quays for many years and now these weakened groins were to be put to the ultimate test.

This is how Jack Hurley described the scene with the help of the press reports of the time: 'In Friday's dawn, to the hammer of the rising tide, Watchet faced the cruellest hour in its maritime history.  No-one who watched would ever forget the scene.  Soon after half-flood the west breakwater crumbled to the terrific pounding, the sea swept through a huge gap, turning the harbour into a maelstrom, and shipowners and seamen watched 12 foot waves remorselessly destroy their vessels and livelihood.'

There were 13 trading vessels in the harbour.  Only three were able to put to sea again.

In his excellent book *Tales of Watchet Harbour* Ben Norman described the scene: 'Mature and tough seamen could be seen on the quay openly weeping as they helplessly watched and heard their beloved ships grinding and groaning in agony as they ripped and tore each other to pieces.

'Four men at great peril to their lives were lowered into a small boat with a view to arresting the drifting craft from the western side of the harbour. The task was beyond them and it was only with extreme difficulty that they were taken off the near sunken boat with ropes.'

Ben has told me: 'This was how I remember my father describing the scene to journalist Will Lee and I can still recall him talking about the terrible grinding and groaning. It really was a blow to those men watching – their entire livelihoods went in just one night.

'The port at Watchet is particularly exposed to westerlies and nor'westerlies – although, oddly enough, it's a sou'westerly which causes the biggest waves. When the wind is blowing hard from the south-west there is real anger in the water.'

Altogether 13 ships faced that angry water early in the morning of 28 December and of them only three survived to sail again – *Electric*, *Forest Deer* and *Commodore*. A further four ships from the Watchet fleet were away at sea, although one of them suffered such a battering in the gale she had to be broken up unsold.

As for the ten wrecks in the harbour – *Express*, *Friends* (two of the same name) *George May*, *Hematite*, *Josephine Marie*, *Mary Lauder*, *Thomasine* and *Mary*, *Sprightly* and *Standard* none were ever to put to sea again and their wrecks were sold off for paltry sums. One, a schooner of 160 tons, fetched just £5 for her salvageable timber while the remains of another were offered free to anyone who would cart them away. The total lot raised £200.

# 4 SNOWFALL
# IN SPRINGTIME

Sir Edward Mountain, Bart., must have thought someone was playing a
foolish April Fools Day joke when told that heavy snow had fallen during
the night on that first day of the month in 1922. But he only had to look
out of the window of his Manor House at Oare to see that the blizzard was
only just beginning to work its way into its stride.

Nevertheless, why be alarmed – the big important meeting of the Eagle,
Star and British Dominions Insurance Company, of which he was chairman and managing director, was not scheduled until 6 April allowing
plenty of time for the unseasonable snow to melt and for him to reach
London.

Sir Edward reached his meeting in time – but only just.

All Saturday 1st the snow kept falling – and on Sunday – and on Monday.
The businessman was now seriously perturbed. He had been getting daily
reports on road conditions and they were anything but good. Come
Monday evening a crisis conference was held at the Manor where it was
agreed that all estate workers as well as other men from the parish would
'dig him out' the next day. If Sir Edward could get off the high hills down
to Porlock, then he would reach London with no further trouble.

Dawn on Tuesday saw fourteen spade-wielding men marching out for a
hard day's work in deep snow – snow which was to close Exmoor's other
roads for a fortnight. In fact, given the size of the drifts they made pretty
good time winning through to Porlock by noon and, according to the *West
Somerset Free Press*, they stayed a while to rest and 'see the sights', whatever that meant, before returning to Oare.

Early the next day Sir Edward mounted his horse and, accompanied by his
son and three guides, made the trek over the hill to Porlock in just three

hours, hiring a car to take him to Taunton and from there to London and his important meeting.

Whether or not the magnate rewarded his hard working 'sherpas' is not known, but the names of the men who knew how to look after their master were: Will Thorne, Harry Thorne, Will Thorne jun., George Thorn, Charlie Thorn, Stanley Moore, Jack Moore, Jack Harding, Jack Squires, Alfred Burge, Victor Martin, Edward Barwick and Fred Down.

As a reminder that spring doesn't necessarily mean the end of winter, it's worth noting that it took a team of 30 men, armed with picks and shovels – armed with a charabanc converted to snowplough – two weeks to clear the roads properly in the Porlock and Oare areas and that the snow was packed so hard in places that shovels were buckled trying to move it.

# 5 THE BLIZZARD BUS

B.B.C. national news the night of Thursday, 28 January, 1937:

A blizzard has been raging over the Westcountry. A public service bus which left Minehead, in Somerset, this afternoon, for Lynmouth, has failed to arrive. Nothing is known of it since it passed through Porlock.

Behind the cool delivery of the newsreader's lines lay a tale of almost epic proportions – and it all started just before 2.30pm when driver Arthur Priddle pulled away into the snow flurries which were swirling thickly down onto the seaside town's bus station.

Passing through the village of Porlock the bus was due to reach Lynton at 4 p.m. after climbing, and descending two of the steepest hills on any road in the country – but needless to say, it failed to arrive at its appointed time.

Arthur Priddle had been nervous about travelling along the high coast road in such conditions and, when he and his four passengers reached the top of infamous Porlock Hill, his worst fears began to materialise. Peering through a windscreen which wipers were failing to clear, driver Priddle thought there was little point in turning back now – they may as well try their luck for Countisbury and the big descent down to sea-level at Lynmouth. As long as he could avoid the rapidly mounting drifts they might stand a chance. Alas Arthur was not to know that the snowfall that afternoon would surpass anything he had before experienced on the hilltop run.

As Jack Hurley reported: 'Where Windwhistle shrieked its name 1374 feet above sea level, Priddle was forced to pull up. And he could not get going again. In ten minutes the water in the radiator froze. It was the end of the road for the little bus.'

It would have been the end of the road for the passengers as well if the driver had not had his wits about him. The bus, which ironically was equipped with a sunshine roof which could be rolled back for summer excursions, was rapidly filling with fine snow. Though the doors and windows were shut it was finding its way in through the seams of this unseasonable fabric roof and Arthur Priddle realised they would have to abandon ship or suffocate in the fine powder.

One passenger, Walter Barnes, fell as he got out and was so badly shaken the five had to retreat back into the vehicle for ten minutes until he revived his spirits. After this they tried again and this time were amazed to find that a car had become stuck in the drift behind them. Its occupants were Mr and Mrs R.H. Penny, of Taunton, and a Mr Cox and they were on their way to a dinner party at Lee Abbey. They agreed with the consensus that it was walk or die – a brave theory when you consider the arctic blizzard conditions which beat and hammered against them at the aptly named Windwhistle.

Poor old Walter Barnes thought it was his end and he told Priddle that there was no way he could make it. But the sturdy bus driver was having none of this defeatist talk and he and a female passenger, Miss Goodwin, took Barnes by the arm and they and a passenger called Snell made their way in the direction of County Gate.

Meanwhile the Pennys, Mr Cox and the fourth bus passenger called Clapp made their way down from the high coast road into the Oare valley towards Lorne Doone Farm where they found shelter and hospitality with Mr and Mrs Albert Richards.

High above, driver Priddle and his three passengers were struggling through the storm and the great drifts as darkness fell.

Out in the great world beyond the snow clad Exmoor plateau, voices of concern were beginning to be raised. Western National Superintendent W.J. Darke had been busy on his telephone at Minehead bus station to no avail. None of the numbers listed for the area around the village of Brendon was answering. Heavy snow had brought down the lines. All he could hope was that the experienced Priddle would lead his passengers to the safety of one of the lonely farmsteads.

*The Blizzard Bus, 1937.* (R. Kingsley Taylor)

*Interior of the snowed up Lynmouth bus.* (R. Kingsley Taylor)

It wasn't until ten the next morning that the wheels of rescue could be put into motion – and this came in the form of an Austin Twelve being driven by Louis Bowden of Dunster. He had been hired to convey the Superintendent as far along the Lynmouth road as his car would travel and the rescue party was to be composed of Mr Darke, W. Toney the depot workshop foreman and Bill Rundle, the *Free Press* reporter who was going along for the story.

They were carrying shovels but soon realised that using these would be futile in any attempt to get up Porlock Hill. Instead Louis Bowden took his Austin up the Toll Road – a journey which Bill Rundle later described as pure adventure.

After this the going was hard work as the passengers constantly had to dig the vehicle through the massive drifts. And eventually even this determined posse had to give up as they came across one 'polar monster' as the huge drift was described.

This meant Superintendent Darke would have to go it alone on foot like some desperate polar explorer. It didn't take him long to find what he was looking for. His company's bus was buried deep in a drift with its bonnet torn off and its engine compartment bunged full with snow. A finer version of the snow he was walking on had also invaded the cabin of the little bus which he checked to see if there were any occupants.

There weren't. Nor were there any tell-tale footprints thanks to the blizzard. The Western National's passengers and driver had disappeared into the white, freezing desert.


Fortunately the refugees from the Minehead-Lynmouth bus had found shelter the previous night at the home of Mr and Mrs Prowsdale and their two children. The frail Walter Barnes had come through the blizzard walk quite well, but Miss Goodwin was overcome and had to be taken to bed. The others warmed themselves by the fire, but it soon became obvious that they had not arrived at the most ideal of sanctuaries. Though the

Prowsdales were kind and welcoming, they only had one bedroom and were simply not provisioned for such an invasion – especially if the blizzard looked set to continue for long.

It wasn't until Saturday morning that the bus driver was able to make contact with his boss at Minehead. Having been told of the situation Darke now returned to the hilltops in Louis Bowden's trusty Austin, accompanied by foreman Toney, and with a boot full of provisions to relieve the passengers and their hosts the Prowsdales. Driving as far as they could, as they'd done the day before, the three men were forced to struggle through breast-high snow to reach the cottage with eggs, bread, butter and brandy.

The passenger Snell returned through freezing rain to the car with them, but it was deemed unwise for Barnes and Miss Goodwin to attempt the walk.

Meanwhile that ever-loyal employee Arthur Priddle was insisting on climbing back up Countisbury to meet the provisioning party, but the sensible folk of Lynmouth managed to dissuade him as it was obvious to them that he'd had enough.

Eventually the two last stranded passengers were brought out of their confinement on Monday when a car was brought along the valley road past Brendon – the high coast road still being impassable.

The fourth passenger Mr Clapp, who had gone down to Lorna Doone Farm with the occupants of the car, said later that he would never forget the experience. On the Friday he had decided to walk into Lynmouth – a journey of 8 miles which took him as many hours.

'It was dreadful,' he said of conditions. 'only better than that of the night before because it was now daylight. But I had to make many detours to avoid gigantic snowdrifts, and I had to walk through the river. How I got to Lynmouth I shall never know. But I do know that I had a merciful escape.'

Bus driver Priddle later said of his party's terrible struggle to the Prowsdale's cottage: 'We were blown about in all directions. I have never seen a blizzard like it. We shall never know how we reached safety.'

# 6 THE FREEZING FORTIES

During the earlier winters of the 1940s Britain was not only suffering the turmoil of the Second World War, it was also in the icy grip of a succession of big freezes. Not that those on the home front were officially allowed to know this – weather reports were censored in case they were of help to a potentially invading enemy.

In January 1940 the people of Exmoor needed no weatherman to tell them that they were suffering the full brunt of the worst winter since 1890-91. Indeed Barnstaple was proclaimed as being colder than at any time since 1881 and the River Taw was frozen above and below Long Bridge.

Other local novel meteorological records were being set with skating being enjoyed on Porlock Marsh for the first time in living memory, while at Mudpool near Brendon, the same sport was being performed for the first time in forty five years. At Court, Exford, a car was driven across the solid ice of the frozen river, and at Withypool an almost frightening temperature reading was taken showing 42 degrees of frost.

As if things weren't grim enough with the big-freeze combining with hardships caused by war, but the weather-gods must step in to exacerbate the misery on Exmoor by dumping not bombs but millions of tons of snow. Snow which some local folk can remember lying up to 18 feet deep in hollows, goyals and lanes.

With the lack of machinery and manpower, conditions were causing all manner of difficulties in remote communities such as Exford and Simonsbath where the situation became bad enough for the setting up of special provisioning parties. Douglas Batchelor, who kept the stores at Exford, put together one such group of volunteers and made the epic journey through the blizzard over to Simonsbath on foot. Each man carrying a full sack on his back, the party departed at ten in the morning and did not return until six that evening. Sixty to seventy loaves were delivered as well as groceries and Douglas said of the adventure:

*The first winter of the war, January, 1940.*

*Near Sticklepath Hill, leading to Brendon Hill, 1940.*

'The fact that there were a good number of us kept us cheerful. The journey would have broken the heart of one man before he had gone half way. The moorland drifts were six to eight feet high, and you could walk over the hedges without knowing they were underneath.'

Meanwhile Simonsbath's sub-postmaster Frank Vigars was having fun all of his own. Frank was a man who believed in delivering the mail come what may, and during the blizzard of 1940 he was known to crawl on hands and knees over frozen drifts, taking five and a half hours for a mail delivery of 7 miles. His daughter summed up the conditions on Exmoor in a newspaper interview at the time:

'My father is walking to Exford and back with one mail a day. The staff are walking over the hedges. It is a change for them not to have to open the gates – for the simple reason that they can't see them!'

Bus driver Arthur Priddle was in the news once more – for exactly the same reason which had found him in the headlines some years earlier. His bus had become stuck in the snow on the Minehead to Lynmouth run again and he'd been forced to abandon her in a drift. However, this time he had no passengers to worry about and, from where he'd come to a grinding halt at the top of Countisbury Hill, he actually could see Lynmouth in its bay far below. Arthur walked down to the little port without having to stay the night in a wayside cottage.

One of the more interesting meteorological phenomenons of this grim winter was the unwelcome occurrence of 'rain-freeze' – a term which quite literally describes the unusual process of rain falling and turning to glassy ice as it descends. The Somerset Archaeological and Natural History Society at the time reported that it: 'Covered every object with a coat of transparent ice. Telegraph wires and twigs were enclosed in ice cylinders sometimes more than an inch in thickness. The air temperature sank to 25 degrees Fahrenheit and did not rise above freezing point for six days.'

'The combined weight of snow and ice caused much damage to wires and trees. The effects have been shown on most upland woods. Large branches were stripped off, and saplings and young trees were snapped of 10 or 12 feet from the ground.  Fast-growing spruce which had been bent over failed to straighten up owing to internal injuries to the fibres.'

Writer Jack Hurley recalled: 'The incessant snapping of over-burdened branches makes it an eerie experience to be out in a rain freeze on a pitch-black night.  In 1940 it was death to the less hardy shrubs and plants. The flowering of wild plants was retarded and at the end of February even such plants as the red deadnettle, lesser celandine, annual poa and chick-weed were flowerless.  But bright scenes were to come - all over the place the dandelion heads made a wonderful show!'

### *The Blizzard of 1947*

Many people insist that 1963 supplied Exmoor with the worst blizzard of the century, but there are those who argue that the mighty snowfalls of '47 amassed themselves into the greatest white-out of the hundred years.

Certainly it was the more miserable.  With the country still in the mean clench of post-war rationing there were far fewer supplies and none of the helpful helicopters which were to service the remote communities sixteen years later.  Nor was the area so well equipped in large powerful snow clearance machines.  The authorities relied on manpower to get things moving, and extremely arduous labour it was according to Williton division highway surveyor Albert Williams who spoke to the press just after the freeze:

'My men have been sheeted in ice.  They have had icicles hanging from their ears and gathering on their eyebrows. Telegraph poles have been iced to double their normal size, and electricity cables have measured 6 inches in diameter.'

He was rebutting criticisms about the long closure of some roads and making the point that muscle-power could do little in the face of such a blizzard even if some of it was supplied by the once mighty German military. There were still prisoners-of-war being held in England at the time and their labour was called upon to help in the crisis.

But, as the first of the snows precipitated onto the lonely villages so the millions of picturesque flakes were to impinge themselves into the memories of hundreds of Exmoor folk who, unaware of the storm that was to follow, were in for some of the whitest weeks of their lives.

One such was a young Luxborough girl called Betty Bown, who was, at the time, attending the village school:

'It snowed thick and fast all morning long and by lunchtime the teacher, Miss Hamilton was worried about us getting home. In those days the milk was brought up to the school, which was near the church in Luxborough, by a lady from a local farm – and I can always remember the teacher heating this up on the stove so that we would have something warm inside us before she sent us home.

'We didn't have too much trouble making our way down over Jumper's Steep, past the pub to where we lived, but we were very glad that we left school when we did. If we had waited until the usual time to go home I'm not sure we'd have ever got there.'

Within hours the lane at Jumper's Steep was filled with snow to the level of its high banks.

Arctic conditions had come in with the New Year and from that date there were 42 days and nights of unrelenting frost with three exceptionally violent blizzards on 28 January, 23 February and 4 March. The last provided the hills with a continuous fall of thirty six hours.

Simonsbath, that most exposed of Exmoor's communities, was in the thick of it once again with postmaster Vigars telling the *Free Press* presumably by phone: 'Things are a bit tight. We shan't get any more supplies until we dig ourselves out. I had five loaves of bread yesterday, but with sharing them out I'm down to one.'

Referring to the rationing he complained: 'In the old days we used to take in about six weeks supplies at Christmas in case the snows came – sacks of flour and yeast. If no meat got through, a farmer would kill a sheep or two and they would be shared out, but you can't do that in these days of ration controls.'

I have an interview on tape which I once recorded with retired estate-worker Stan Curtis who has lived in or near Simonsbath all his life, and he recalled: 'In 1947 we were clearing snow up here on Gallon House Plain between Simonsbath and Exford and I was working nights and I was clearing the same piece of road as the other bloke working the bulldozer who'd work it by day – and this went on – must have been two months. What happened was we'd do the same piece of road because it would keep blowing in and blocking the road up all over again.

'That was the longest I can remember being cut-off up here at Simonsbath – must have been getting on toward thirteen weeks before any traffic came in. Well, we weren't properly cut-off because a gang of us would walk in to Exford to get the provisions. Back in those days there wasn't any electric up here, no deep-freezes and the like. Not like the stuff we've got nowadays when you think to yourself – right, 'tis autumn, let's fill up the freezer so we're ready for it if the snow comes.

'Anything that was kept then was packed in salt and such like. Well there's a limitation to what you can do with that.'

I asked Stan if it took a different sort of person to spend a lifetime up in the wilds of one Exmoor's highest and remote villages: 'I think it helps to be somebody that's bit tough and doesn't know any better,' he laughed.

It certainly takes a different sort of person to carry out potentially life-threatening tasks when, in the great scheme of things, it might seem more sensible to wait until the danger is over. Elsewhere on the Brendon Hills that excellent if not old-fashioned principle of doing one's duty come what may was being executed by many hard-working inhabitants. One such was my grandfather Harold Langsford who made the newspaper headlines at the time for his herculean efforts to deliver the mail on his 25-mile round across the hills.

First an early dose of snow and ice caused him to crash his motorcycle and sidecar at the bottom of Ford Hill near Wiveliscombe and, despite several injuries including a broken finger, he walked into town to begin his long country round. Then, after a couple of weeks in bed under doctor's orders, he returned to his job just in time for the big dump of snow. That meant walking to Wiveliscombe from his Stogumber home, and then embarking on his 25-mile round mostly on foot.

'I had heard the old folk talking about being able to walk over gates and hedge-tops in the snow, but I had never really believed it until then,' he told one newspaper which carried a graphic account of my grandfather almost perishing in deep snow near Skilgate and only managing to extricate himself with the help of his postbag which had caught on something solid during his fall.

'Many were the bacon and egg breakfasts, the roast pork dinners and the hot drinks received beneath the hospitable roofs of the Brendons,' reported the newspaper.

One of the more unusual bad-weather tales caused by the '47 blizzards occurred when two young men serving in the RAF were sent onto Exmoor to guard a crashed plane. Little did they know when they took up their lonely posts that a blanket of deep snow would soon be threatening their lives.

The plane had crashed near Larkbarrow and on Tuesday, 28 January two young airmen, equipped with a truck, a coal brazier and some rations, drove up onto the moor from their base at RAF Chivenor. That night the blizzard struck and youth and inexperience combined to very nearly make an end of the two guards.

Fine powdery snow had found its way into the truck and covered their supply of coal, so they were unable to get the brazier going. As the tem-

45

perature plummeted so their rations froze – as did anything they might drink.

By Thursday things looked dire indeed for the two young men who had not had a drink since Tuesday and were in the last stages of dying from exposure. Luckily for them officers from their base had, on the Thursday morning, phoned Exford police station asking if a rescue mission might be mounted.

In fact mounted turned out to be the right description for the rescue as PC Trott and Special Constable Frank Mullins set out on horseback in an attempt to break through the deep snow. But eventually the horses had to be abandoned at Wellshead Farm and the two continued on foot.

PC Trott said later: 'The plane was about three miles away, but we trudged about six in trying to get to it, because we were coming up against snow eight feet deep.'

In the aftermath of this ferocious winter many Exmoor voices were raised in disapprobation aimed at anyone and everything empowered to react to such freak conditions. The NFU, estimating a 33 per cent loss of sheep wintering above an altitude of 600 feet, was out for justice when it came to compensation, and it was also putting much of the blame on the Air Ministry's (the Met. Office of the day) forecasters who announced a thaw just before the third and most ferocious blizzard. This mistake, according to the NFU, caused Exmoor farmers the loss of more than 1000 sheep because, being desperately short of feed, they had turned animals out onto the common prematurely.

# 7  DELUGE AND TRAGEDY: THE LYNMOUTH FLOOD DISASTER

By far the worst, most tragic, single weather incident ever to hit the region occurred on the night of 15/16 August, 1952, when more than 90 million tons of water cascaded down the steep narrow valleys towards Lynmouth causing death and devastating destruction as it swept towards the sea.

In all 34 people lost their lives that black night and as day eventually dawned so its light revealed what was left of a once pretty seaside village, now looking more like something from the Second World War blitz.

During the night one eye-witness, making his way to safety across rooftops, watched as cars, buildings and whole trees swept by just feet away from him in a torrent which had turned the modest stream into a giant as wide as the Thames at Tower Bridge.

It comes as no surprise to learn that all this devastation was caused by one of the heaviest rainfalls to have ever been recorded in the British Isles.

A rain gauge kept by a local meteorologist on the high moors close to Longstone Barrow showed that between mid-morning on the 15th and 9 a.m. on the 16th ,9 inches of rain fell on the central plateau of Exmoor. That puts this single precipitation into the record books – such a fall has only ever been equalled twice in the British Isles.

What's more incredible is that most of the 9 inches fell between 7pm and midnight!

It was this final, torrential downpour – estimated to have been more than 3000 million gallons on The Chains alone – which filled the great peat bogs of Exmoor to overflowing. It had been raining perpetually and heavily for two weeks, but this last deluge was too much for the already sodden moors. There was nowhere else for the water to go but down – off the hill.

Down the East and West Lyn Valleys to the north, and down the Exe and the Barle to the south and east.

When talking of the Lynmouth Flood Disaster, as it's always referred to, the incredible devastation caused along the banks of these other rivers is rarely discussed – perhaps because, miraculously, there was no loss of human life. Nevertheless, there are extraordinary stories told by those who escaped the floods and we'll be hearing some of these later.

But first we must look at the events that concurred to produce the night of terror at Lynmouth, the sleepy, picturesque village, beloved by the poet Southey and with, at the time, a resident population of 450 which had swelled with holidaymakers that fateful August, to more than 1200.

Even its name gives us a clue to the fate of the place. Llynna comes from the Anglo-Saxon and means torrent – so that Lynmouth is the 'town on the torrent'.

But far more sinister omens than an ancient appellation began to appear on that wet Friday. One observer at the time remarked how he saw a heavy bank of clouds, unusually dark and tinged with deep red and purple, making its way slowly from west to east. Strangely and ominously there was another ceiling of cloud passing underneath at fast speed — in the opposite direction!

At 1pm there was an extremely heavy downpour which several local people remarked upon because the sky seemed to take on a weird, uncanny appearance. The rain then fell steadily all afternoon until 5pm when another extreme fall began. By then it was getting dark –- not at all usual for an August evening – but as yet no-one was alarmed even though the rivers were in high spate.

The first portent that may have caused foreboding in those that had to deal with it was that the floods had damaged the canal leading to the hydro-electric plant which powered the two isolated communities of Lynton and Lynmouth. This was at 7.30pm and a switch-over to the diesel plant allowed supplies to be maintained until 9pm when water began to find its way into the flywheels causing a shut-down. At that moment the villages were plunged into darkness.

Later the engineer C.H. Postles and his assistant R.N. Freeman were commended for their courage and adherence to duty for keeping supplies going for as long as they did despite risking their lives in the rising flood.

By 8.30pm the Police Station telephone was beginning to heat up. Calls were coming in with reports of flooded, impassable roads. The first appeals for help were made and a fire-tender was despatched to Radsbury Farm where a dam had burst. A second tender, manned by six part-time firemen accompanied by P.C. Harper, began a journey to the hamlet of Bridgeball, a mile or so beyond Hillsford Bridge above Watersmeet. It never reached its destination, horrified by the scene illuminated in their headlights at Hillsford Bridge, the crew realised they must return as fast as the tender would take them. They later described the hour-long trip back which, in normal circumstances it would have taken just a few minutes, as 'nightmarish'.

Upon reaching the first houses in Lynmouth they now found themselves marooned on the land between the East and West Lyn Rivers. Pondering their next move they heard cries for help and the policeman and two firemen made their way into one of the dwellings, only to find a woman struggling in 5 feet of water. She was rescued but minutes later it was P.C. Harper's turn to escape from the jaws of death.

He was determined to get back to Lynton so that he could be of use in what was obviously becoming an emergency situation, and he began to make his way across the flooded bridge with a rope around his middle just in case. Before he'd proceeded more than a quarter way across the rope was needed. The crew on the bank had become aware of a terrifying roar

49

emanating from up river and they didn't wait to find out what was causing it – they rudely hauled the policeman back from his travels. Within moments a wall of water and debris came down the narrow valley smashing the bridge as if it were made of matchsticks.

It was about 10.30pm and this violent surge, coming down the valley with all the horrifying strength of a tidal wave, gives us some clue as to why the disaster became such a tragedy. Had the waters simply risen smoothly to their maximum flood it may have been that fewer lives were lost. But who could have expected these deadly surges? They were caused it seems, by the waters building up behind an obstacle such as a bridge and flooding rapidly as debris such as trees and boulders began to collect. Eventually the sheer weight and force of the flood would burst through the blockage in one violent wave. This surge would then pass down to the next obstacle where the same would happen again causing another, even greater wave to sweep away once the blockage was overcome.

This pattern of blockage and surge would naturally increase as the rivers descended the steep valleys, so by the time a wave hit Lynmouth it would be at its largest and be carrying its greatest load of debris.

Another tale of the build up to these extraordinary floods was later recounted by John Loosemore, a Lynmouth man who beheld, with the aid of the lightning that ripped the sky, a new sea. It was Brendon Common.

He had been driving some people home to the village of Brendon and had noticed on his way the swollen river bringing down rocks and tress, blocking Lyndale Bridge. When he tried to find his way back Hillsford Bridge had gone. He made for Rockford but found that another bridge had collapsed. Then came a vain attempt to return via Simonsbath. Returning to Rockford he tried to telephone but there was no contact.

John Loosemore sat in his car all night hearing the terror of the crashing, roaring rivers, but not being able to see a thing in the pitch black. 'I have never experienced anything so terrifying. I heard the rattling of boulders as they were washed down the river, and the crashing of torn up trees and branches.'

At daybreak he attempted to reach Lynmouth by going around Simonsbath and Challacombe, but when he got to Exe Head the road was hidden by masses of earth and heather. Once more Mr Loosemore turned back to Rockford. Leaving his car he spent hours going through woods and climbing hills. Eventually he reached the foot of Countisbury Hill, but was in no better situation; the floods barred his way home.

Perhaps Mr Loosemore had a lucky escape. As he sat in his car safely on the hillside, neighbours of his were dying in their homes.

At Middleham just half a mile up river from Lynmouth ten cottages were about to become nothing more than the fabric of history. In one of these a visitor staying with the Ritch family asked in the early evening if anyone had seen the river so high before. That was at 8.15pm and he was told it was nothing to worry about. By 8.30pm they were carrying furniture upstairs and just minutes later they wisely decided to abandon the house.

They were joined by the residents of eight of the other houses, but one remained occupied. Elderly Mr and Mrs W.H. Watts and her seventy-eight-year-old brother Mr G. Litson, decided they were going to bed despite warnings and pleas from the neighbours. Not long after the refugees had climbed up to the school where they were to spend the night, they heard a great roar and looking down could see their homes engulfed in an awesome torrent. In an agony of helplessness they watched as the bedroom light of the only occupied house flickered out in the flood.

The angry waters of Exmoor had taken the first three lives.

At 1.20am a deafening roar was heard as an enormous surge ripped down through the gorge engulfing everything that stood before it. After it had passed the only evidence that ten cottages had so recently stood by the river was a sign that swung in a tree opposite the road advertising 'bed and breakfast'.

Further down the Watersmeet Road another group of cottages were in the firing line. It was nearly 10pm when the four homes known as Bevan's

51

Cottages began to take the brunt of the flood when a tree smashed through the bolted and barred door belonging to the Rudall family. Within seconds their other outside door gave way and Mr Rudall knew that it was time to leave. He carried a young grandson to a high wall at the back of the house and returned for his wife. Staggering neck deep in the flood they were making their way back to the wall and safety when they heard neighbour Bill Richards shouting for help from his bedroom window.

'Get us help, the houses are going,' the man screamed. But for him, his wife and two young children, it was too late. Within minutes the houses collapsed in the raging waters and none of the family were ever seen again.

At about this time Mr F.W. Bale, the local traffic warden, and his family were making a dangerous journey across the roof of their garage. At Vale Cottages where they lived the same thing had happened – a tree had smashed through the door to let in the flood. This perilous rooftop journey was their only means of escape and fortunately they made it to safety.

A mile away on the West Lyn at Barbrook more death and destruction was about to occur. Here a row of ten council houses may have been regarded as being high enough above the river to be safe from the deluge. In normal times they stood some 30 feet above the water level but on this freak night their walls were soon to be underneath the flood.

Twelve of their occupants were doomed.

Fred Floyd peered out into the darkness at about 9.30pm to find, to his horror, that the river had risen 30 feet since the afternoon. The road at the front of the house had itself turned into a river and Fred knew they were in trouble. His first thoughts were to get his bedridden mother out of the house and he called to his father to lend a hand.

That was the last thing Fred ever did. Within a second of his asking for help the house simply disintegrated and eight of its inhabitants were lost to the flood.

Freakishly, given the tumultuous raging of torrent and debris, one member of the family survived. Sixty three year-old Tom Floyd later recalled his son asking for help just seconds before the walls caved in. Hurled through black depths of water Mr Floyd managed to grab some masonry which allowed him to regain his feet, although he was unable to fight against the force of water which pushed him down the road. Fortunately his daughter (who lived a few doors down) had made it to safety and was able to reach out and catch him before he was swept into oblivion. His survival was regarded as being nothing short of a miracle – as was the fact that his Cairn terrier also managed to escape the flood.

Other residents of the council houses were also in trouble. One of them, kindly Mrs Ridd who had taken in two rain-soaked Australian girls for the night, was struggling to escape the flood with her eight-year-old grandson. It is believed that they were both sucked into a huge hole which the flood had gouged out of the road.

As for the Australian hikers, twenty-two-year-old Gwenda Oxley and twenty-one-year-old Joyce Hiscock, they fared no better. Their bodies were later found, but in what terrifying circumstances they drowned no-one will ever know.

Survivors from the Barbrook council houses had some disquieting stories to tell. Mr and Mrs Jenkins (a son-in-law and daughter of Mr Floyd) knew that something was amiss when filthy brown water ran out of their taps. With plenty of fresh water falling from the skies they dragged a tin bath outside to collect what they could – only to see it disappear into the black night in a rush of flood. This surreal warning occurred just in time for them to escape.

Sixteen year-old Roy Williams, baby-sitting his two brothers in another of the houses, showed a cool decisive mind when he watched as the kitchen wall dissolved into the night. He rushed through to the front of the house where he told thirteen year-old Morris to pass their sleeping three-year-old brother John out through the window to him. All three were able to make their escape.

Unlike their little friend Kenneth Bowen, aged nine – one of the members of the Floyd household who died in the flood. His broken body was later found trapped under a butcher's slab down at Lynmouth which, in a macabre way, illustrated to those who found him the awesome force of that terrible flood.

Down where the two steep, almost gorge-like valleys met at Lynmouth, holidaymakers and locals alike were undergoing a night of terror which none of them would ever forget. At the famous Lyndale Hotel 40 guests, as well as members of staff and family of owner, eighty-year-old Tom Bevan, were huddled in upstairs rooms wondering how much more of a battering the thick walls could take.

Earlier Mr Bevan had called the fire brigade to request that they come and pump out his flooded cellars. They never arrived and soon no-one cared about the state of the basement – they were too concerned with the floods which were sweeping through the lower floors.

Luckily for them the builders who had constructed the Lyndale Hotel had done a first-class job. For the structure withstood the tremendous onslaught that night even though it was situated at the very point where the two wild rivers met. In fact one wing housing the billiard and other rooms did succumb to the pounding, but the main building stood solid even though several 15 ton boulders as well as trees and other debris, built up a 30 foot-high bank of rubble against its walls.

Part of this debris was provided by the chapel, the fruit shop and a garage which were all demolished. In fact the four occupants of the fruit shop were washed against the walls of the Lyndale as they tried to escape, and would have been drowned if they hadn't been able to attract the attention of those inside who helped haul them up to safety. To rescue one, a Mrs Pavey who was rapidly losing her grip on the iron railings she was clutching for dear life, a man had to be lowered from a window by others who held onto his legs. Within in minutes of fishing her out there was no sign of the railings as the rising waters enveloped them.

Safety might be too solid a word to describe the conditions inside the hotel. As the boulders and trees crashed into its sides the very fabric of the building shuddered and groaned. As they huddled in their blankets, the frightened occupants could only wince with fear each time a crash heralded what must have seemed like an inevitable end. Imagine that candle-lit gloom, occasionally brilliantly illuminated by a fierce flash of lightning, where people could barely hear each other shout because of the tremendous roar of the flood. A roar which, at around 1am, became horrendously loud when, it's believed, the remains of Bevan's Cottages must have crashed into the flanks of the hotel.

The agonising suspense ended for the frightened inmates with the arrival of a uniformed policeman who almost magically appeared in one of the upstairs windows. Somehow P.C. Harper had climbed the debris thrown high up against the wall of the hotel by the now ebbing flood and, as the first light of dawn began to glow reluctantly, so the guests and staff found that evacuation was now possible. There was only one way out and that was by the same route as the policeman had arrived.

He and firemen friends had been doing sterling work throughout the night. Between them they rescued some 30 people from flooded buildings, including one elderly woman who was bed-ridden and paralysed.

These people were still stranded between the two rivers and Harper was determined to make contact with the outside world to bring in help. In the grey light of dawn he saw that the ebbing floods had dropped enough to reveal the parapet of the bridge on the A39 Porlock road and, with almost crazy courage, he straddled this wall and with his feet dangling in the raging water, crossed safely to the Tors Hotel where some 150 people huddled in sleepless horror. The phones were not working so the gallant policeman requisitioned a car and drove through thick fog to Porlock to raise the alarm. He was later awarded the George Medal for his courageous work.

On the other side of the river, in the main village of Lynmouth, the onslaught of the floods had taken everyone by horror and surprise. The main street became a funnel channelling a torrent of floodwater and debris and it seems almost unbelievable that into this seven lady holidaymakers elected to make their escape. They had been enjoying the Summer Show at the Pavilion when the lights went out and put an end to the entertainment. And making their exit they, like other members of the audience, were appalled to find the streets in flood as the dreadful reality of the night hit them. But unlike the rest of the crowd, they inexplicably turned their backs on the safety of Mars Hill and, linking arms, marched into the flood to make their way towards the Lyn Valley Hotel. Six of them miraculously survived but one, a fifty-six-year-old Miss Cherry from London, slipped and before her friends could help her, was washed away in the flood. Her body was found at Clovelly weeks later.

At the same moment one of her companions was also swept away, but had a very lucky escape when, being funnelled down the main street, she grabbed at the wheel of an ambulance. In an instant the driver Supt. C.A. Durman, was able to reach out and save her although he could only watch as poor Miss Cherry continued her fateful journey to the sea.

In the same lethal area three residents of the Lyn Valley Hotel – two women and a man – also lost their lives in the flood.

Meanwhile, over at the Lyn Valley Hotel, 50 people were trapped in upstairs rooms expecting the end to overtake them at any moment. Their fears were greatly heightened when the hotel's tower which faced the river was battered down by one of the mighty surges sweeping down the valley. In fact this was partly responsible for their eventual escape as the loud crash it made drew the attention of rescue parties who by this time were hard at work. A frail bridge was put across Granny's Lane from the cliff to an upstairs room and the rescue party, including medical officer Dr M.P. Nightingale, inched their way across to the frightened occupants – each and everyone of whom were then conveyed across what was no more than a ladder to safety. A fearful crossing it must have been just feet above a lane which was now a deadly sluice, with the only illumination emanating from candles and the occasional flash of lightning.

This same rescue party went on to save many other lives with extraordinary courage – often resorting to the same tactics of crossing by ladder from the steep, cliff-like, hill to the rear of the buildings.

Other rescue operations were being effected by P.C.s Earle and Pavey – both of whom received the British Empire Medal for their work that night. P.C. Pavey continued to battle on even though he was frightened for the safety of his wife, whose rescue from the iron railings outside the Lyndale Hotel has already been mentioned.

The postmaster Mr Pedder was another who put the call of duty above thoughts of personal safety. With his son John he had gone down to the Post Office to save valuable documents when the pair of them became trapped in a small back-room. The schoolboy kept a cool head and smashed a skylight so that he and his father could climb across roofs to safety.

Forty-five years later John Pedder told me: 'The strangest thing up on that roof was watching as cars rushed by in the flood. The batteries had shorted or something because all their head-lights were blazing which made the whole scene unreal as the cars rolled over and over in the water.'

Nearby another shopkeeper was faring a little better. For some reason the premises of fruiterer S.C. Willshere were being protected from the worst ravages of the flood by the way in which surrounding buildings deflected the waters. Indeed his telephone link with the outside world was the only one left operative in the stricken village and so he was able to deliver a running commentary on conditions to the people organising rescue services up the hill in Lynton. It is said that Mr Willshere remained calm throughout but remained hotly adamant on one point only – that should rescuers ever manage to get through to him they in no way should forget to bring him a fresh supply of cigarettes...

*These remarkable pictures of Lynmouth were taken by Dr M. P.*
*Nightingale in the early hours following the devastating flood.*

One of the people he had been in contact with was Mr W.H. Tall who, as Civil Defence controller for the area, had set up an emergency centre in the Valley of Rocks Hotel. Down at the bottom of Mars Hill the famous Rising Sun Hotel, with the waters now lapping at its doorstep, became another hostelry given over to the rescue operation with gangs of brave volunteers using the place as a base.

Meanwhile two elderly ladies living in separate cottages just above Watersmeet Road, slept on impervious to the hellish scenes occurring just outside their bedroom windows. The next morning both Miss Mary and Miss Alice Crocombe thought they had 'gone potty' (as they put it) when daylight revealed to them a view of the sea which they never seen from their windows before. The cottages and buildings opposite the road which had obscured the vista were now gone. They were the last Lynmouth residents to be evacuated and even then were reluctant to go.

There is little point in describing the scene which daylight revealed after that terrible night. The black and white news photographs describe the devastation much more succinctly than words.

Suffice to say that 28 of the area's bridges were no more, many buildings had totally disappeared including the well known star of many a post-card – the Rhenish Tower (later rebuilt in every detail). The numbers of badly damaged structures were beyond count which isn't surprising given that an estimated 100,000 tons of boulders had been washed down the valleys like twigs in a stream. 121 motor vehicles were salvaged from the ruins and the sea while 18 boats were counted as being lost.

Some idea of the scouring action of the great flood can be gleaned from the fact that partially filled petrol tanks buried deep under the tarmac at Lynmouth had been clawed from their foundations never to be seen again.

Rest centres were set up and the people of Lynton whose homes had survived undamaged opened their doors to the evacuees. Soldiers, RAF men and County Council workers by the hundreds were drafted in. The gigan-

tic job of putting Lynmouth back on the map had begun with commend-
able efficiency by mid-morning.

## *Havoc Elsewhere on Exmoor*

With such tragic loss of life Lynmouth rightly took the spotlight of world
attention during the aftermath of the disaster. But deaths did occur elsewhere and people living in many other villages on Exmoor had terrifying
experiences of a flood they'd never forget.

Parracombe had one of the most frightening incidents when a tidal wave
hit the village in the middle of the evening. The waters of the River
Heddon had become trapped behind a 50 foot embankment when a
number of culverts choked – and when the flood eventually broke through
the village, just under a mile away, was directly in the firing line. The
wave hit the community's little bridge with such force that it shattered into
pieces and few parts of it were ever seen again. Customers at the Fox and
Goose Inn had a shock as they watched the waters cover the bar in a
matter of seconds.

But it was the second torrent which hit the place just after midnight that
was responsible for the taking of lives. Sixty-year-old Mr W.J. Leaworthy
had gone out for a second time to check on his sister. His body was later
found a mile away in a mass of debris.

At Mill Farm Mrs A. Thorne from Surrey, and her fourteen-year-old son
were asleep in a holiday chalet which was entirely swept away in the
flood. Their bodies were later found downstream.

One of the most poignant and tragic episodes in this catalogue of disaster
occurred at Shallowford, near Filleigh. Here in the meadows a troop of
Manchester Boy Scouts had made their camp and it was during the early
hours that they awoke to find their tents completely awash. Most scrambled through the flood to safety, but four boys were missing. The scout-
master, with no thought of the danger, waded back and was carried 60
yards downstream where he found just one of the boys clinging to the

branches of a tree. Together they were able to struggle to safety – but the other three scouts were lost. Their bodies were found later.

Closer to The Chains, from which much of the floodwater had come, our old friend Simonsbath postmaster Frank Vigars, was up to his neck in it again. Simonsbath was flooding fast and Frank was appalled to find his wife and two grandchildren floating about the kitchen on a table. He carried them to the safety of the woodshed higher up the hill.

Stan Curtis has recalled his memories of that grim black night: 'Myself, my brother and my brother-in-law had been racing our motorbikes up Porlock Hill and we had a job getting back with all the water across the road. But we were amazed at how much chaos we found back here at Simonsbath. There was obviously some sort of problem at the Exmoor Forest Hotel, there were no lights. Mr Holman, who was the owner, shouted out the window, "For God's sake help us, we're all going to drown."

'Well, the river had come down from Ashcombe Bottom and it was going into the back of the hotel and couldn't come out of the front. It had come up above the dining room windows and everyone was upstairs – of course, being August the place was full of guests. The windows were all holding back the water and we wondered what we could do. So we went through and smashed the windows and let a lot of water out.

'But then I said, "us have got to smash the front door down – but how are we going to do it without being washed away?"

'We decided that we'd go around and shut the garden gates in the front, so that if we got washed away they would stop us. Anyway, being young and foolish we smashed the door down and soon as we broke the door a bit he smashed all to pieces and we were washed down to the garden gates.

'It might sound a bit big headed but we three saved that hotel – it (the flood) would have eventually brought the front wall out because it's a very old building.

'There was flood relief money and some people got new cars. But I got nothing except for three and sixpence for having my suit cleaned.'

Later the three young men shared a bottle of rum they found in the bar to try and warm themselves from the hours they had spent wet to the skin, but even the entire bottle failed to instil any comfort to their chilled bones.

At roughly the same time another motorcyclist was heading for Simonsbath. P.C. E.J. Hutchings of Exford was making his way across the moor to investigate a reported landslide which was blocking the road. But, fortunately as it turned out for Exford and for that matter Dulverton, he never made it to the subsidence.

Riding through torrential rain P.C. Hutchings was wet enough as it was, but he was not expecting to be hurled from his machine by a solid wall of water. Lying unscathed in the middle of the road the policeman could hardly believe what had just occurred, but looking through the rain at the flooding hills and valleys from his vantage point, he realised one thing – Exford and the other villages must be warned! A surge was coming down the river valley and he calculated that by coasting his now dead machine back down the steep hill he could just make it to the phone at the White Horse Hotel in time to send out the alarm.

Minutes later the soaked constable was standing ankle deep in the bar which was already beginning to flood. Four minutes later it was up to his chest. But the all-important phone calls had been made. Dulverton was now on the alert.

Across the bar in the hotel's office licensee's wife Mrs Rolfe was trying to salvage what she could with her daughter Eileen. Pound notes might have been floating about the place but it was soon realised that the only safe place was upstairs. Outside Mr Rolfe's car was being wrenched from its garage by the waters, and dragged across the recreation ground to the river.

Just over the road elderly Dick Steer was clinging to the picture rail. The bedridden old man lived downstairs in a cottage where now waters were approaching ceiling height. Luckily Mr Steer's bed was floating and the old fellow was rescued just in time by his son Robert and a friend, Henry Perry.

Nearby beekeeper Alec Meadows was checking on his hives – to little avail. Both they and he were washed away by the floods. Luckily Mr Meadows was able to grab a tree branch after a dizzying rush of 100 yards, and somehow managed to haul himself to safety. In one major rescue operation eight valuable horses were freed from Frank Mullins' rapidly flooding stables. By 10.42pm Somerset Police Headquarters were to receive the following laconic message from the constables of Exford, which in a few brief words managed to sum the situation neatly up: 'Cloudburst. Telephone kiosk submerged.'

A mile or so down river at Nethercote farm, mother of four 'Buster' Johnson was just beginning a new life on Exmoor with her husband Johnny and she recorded the night in a fascinating diary which she kept over many years and which marvellously recounts life in this lonely corner of the hills:

'Even the Exe turned into a roaring seething wall of water which came hurtling down from the moor. It swept away everything it encountered, bulldozing trees and flattening high earth banks topped by hedges, carrying away chicken houses with birds inside and the tents of a scout camp, engulfing corn crops and village gardens and flooding houses in Exford and Winsford...'

Mrs Johnson describes how she spent a worried night listening to the rain, waiting for her husband and farm-hand Arthur to return from a trip to the end of the lane to pick up a plumber and some sacks of cement. By dawn they had yet to arrive and she made her way to the side of the bank where she could survey the valley:

'There was no river to be seen, no bridge across the place where the river should have been, no lane leading to Larcombe Foot on the other side of the bridge. Just a vast ocean of turgid brown water which had swallowed up everything and was reaching two-thirds of the way up the meadow towards the house...

'I ran upstairs and woke the children and we gazed awe-struck, at the amazing sight. We appeared to be totally cut off from the outside world.

'The men finally turned up at 10.30am having walked down from the top of the farm. Johnny told us he had reached Larcombe Foot in the van without trouble. The river was running high as it always does after heavy rain, but was well within its banks. They soon had the bags of cement loaded, collected the plumber and set off up the lane homeward bound.

'But they hadn't gone far before, without warning, a rearing wall of water travelling down the valley like an immense tidal wave swallowing up river, river bank and road came rushing towards them. Johnny instantly shot the gears into reverse and fled backwards before it, but it was moving too fast and soon swirled around the van, swamping the wheels and lapping through the floorboards. All he could do was back the van up quickly onto a piece of higher ground and hope it wouldn't be swept away.

'They scrambled out and up the hillside out of harm's way and so back to the bridge at the end of the lane which they'd left only minutes before. But the great wall of water had already reached it and carried it away like chaff.'

Johnny Johnson was determined to get back up to the farm to save stock which he knew to be in the water-meadows, but after many wet, nocturnal adventures which included almost drowning in the torrent, he returned to the van where he spent a shivering night huddled with the others. At dawn the waters dropped sufficiently for them to cross the river by crawling across the remaining girders of the bridge on all fours.

'Later that day,' wrote Mrs Johnson, 'we walked along the high water mark left by the receding river and gathered some of the flotsam which had come down from Exford. We found a whole sheaf of bills and accounts from the office of an Exford firm, and subsequently returned them, but the blacksmith lost all his accounts and had no idea how many horses he had shod or what bolts and bearings and ploughshares and other farm requirements he had fashioned in his forge. We all had to rack our brains to remember the occasions on which we had required his services.

'The saddler had his entire stock of harness and leather goods carried away and we found some of it on our banks. We also picked up garden tools, a wellington boot and a jar full of nutmegs... We also heard that, next morning, a trout was found swimming around in someone's kitchen sink.'

Mrs Johnson notes how the ground floors of all riverside cottages in Winsford were flooded to ceiling level, including the vicarage where parish records dating back centuries had to be meticulously aired to save them.

Nethercote is on the River Exe, but just across the hill at 10.40pm on the night of the deluge, the picturesque village of Withypool was suffering from the anger of the Barle. Eye-witnesses claimed the 20 foot-wide river increased its girth to almost 100 yards during the night. Many houses were flooded, although there were no fatalities. The local newspaper noted one of the flood story's more ironic snippets in its extensive coverage: 'A prayer book was found floating in a flooded room. It was open at a passage from the baptismal service... "Almighty and everlasting God, who by Thy great mercy didst save Noah and his family from perishing by water, and didst safely lead the children of Isreal through the Red Sea..." '

Further downstream the beauty spot at Tarr Steps was still calmly innocent of the maelstrom that was about to hit it. At that time A.W. Cruickshank, of the Tarr Steps Hotel, was crossing the famous clapper bridge. Within just twenty minutes the ancient monument ceased to exist. Just one of its stones remained in place the rest being washed away to be collected, numbered and re-erected at a later date.

Downstream again at Dulverton P.C. Hutchings' warning 'phone call had brought the authorities to a state of readiness. Not that much could be done to save property in the face of such forces but at least the locals were not caught in their beds. And here we have another clue as to the time-scale of events. Just after 11 pm, when the clapper bridge some 5 miles up-river had disappeared, Charles Abbot – chairman of Dulverton RDC – was crossing an as yet unflooded town bridge. Before midnight the bridge had been broadsided by a 15 foot wall of water which careered about causing mayhem across the lower areas of the town.

Once again it was the uprooted trees which were to do most damage to property. The Golden Guernsey Milk Bar, close to the bridge, had simply disappeared by the time daylight revealed the extent of devastation – and it's occupants could count themselves as being some of the luckiest people to be alive. That night the milk bar's caretaker Mrs E. Heard, was being visited by her son Clive, her daughter Mrs G. Bryant and her two-year-old grandson Jeremy as well as another family of three guests. They were forced to smash a hole in the roof of the building to escape. It was lucky for them that they did so. The entire premises collapsed at 2am.

A neighbouring garage was robbed of its cars by the flood which replaced them with trees. Nearby the Boot and Bridge Inns were both badly damaged.

The next day carrots and other vegetables from Dulverton gardens were to be seen hanging forlornly high in trees miles downstream. Harmless casualties of a great and terrifying storm which, on this side of Exmoor at least, had done its violent worst – miraculously without taking human life...

# 8  THE BLIZZARD OF 1962-63

About 12 per cent of the Earth's surface is permanently covered by snow and ice, and in late December, through January, February and early March of this infamous winter, the people of Somerset and Devon, and Exmoor in particular, must have thought the region was about to join the eight million square miles that lie beneath this chilly statistic.

For most people of my age or over, '63 was 'the big one' and I well remember the thrill – and the chill – of this extraordinary freeze which prevented us West Somerset kids from attending school and sent us happily sledding in the steepest fields to which we could wade. Meanwhile the grown-ups were having a far more serious time of it fighting with what was arguably the deepest snow of the century.

My father was out and about dodging far bigger drifts than me – some up to 30 feet in height – in order to cover the snow story for his paper the *Somerset County Gazette*, and much of this chapter comes from his cuttings file.

It all began as the Old Year went out with a bang. Late in the evening of Saturday, 29 December, 1962 an east wind, 'blew a banshee note at the keyholes,' according to Jack Hurley. 'And then the snowbag was ripped from side to side.'

'This was the snow siege of Somerset. All western counties wore the white and weighty shroud, but all except Somerset had some free areas. Over Somerset the spread had missed not a sector of town or acre of countryside...'

On Monday H.S. Holman, the proprietor of the Exmoor Forest Hotel at Simonsbath, was sending out an SOS message requesting a food delivery for the village. And the next day an RAF helicopter obliged by flying the first of many mercy missions which would keep the crews busy for months.

By the end of the week front page coverage in the *Somerset County Gazette* put it this way: 'Again and again the men in the RAF helicopters have risked their lives to drop fodder and food supplies to remote farms on Exmoor and the Quantocks. But for this many families would now be faced with the gravest hardship.'

Farmer M.A. Bucknall, of Triscombe House, near Crowcombe, on the Quantocks was among them. He had a large number of sheep out on the top of the hills and he was unable to reach them by tractor and so called the RAF for help.

'Again and again the helicopter, carrying ten bales at a time, flew low over the flocks on the south side of the Quantocks from St Audries to Bagborough, and Mr Bucknall had the satisfaction of seeing at least a proportion of his animals fed,' reported Peter Hesp.

Farmer Bucknall had told him: 'It was unbelievable up there. In places snow had drifted 20 feet deep, nearly burying whole plantations. Even quite large trees were only sticking up through the snow like little bushes.'

At the same time helicopters were dropping food supplies and fodder to farms on Exmoor, including Lillycombe, the home of the Earl of Lytton. Close to the house a powerful bulldozer had been literally stopped in its tracks by the snow and before the telephone lines had been brought down by the weight of ice and drifts, Lord Lytton had made a call appealing for mechanics to come out to try and start the machine.

In Tuesday's deep snow a team from Gliddons, the Williton agricultural engineers, went out in a tractor and a Land Rover to try and answer this call, but were only able to get as far as Porlock's Toll Road.

'Next day,' reported the press, 'in spite of warnings about an impending blizzard, two of the men, Mr Derek Mattravers and Mr Frank Winter, both of them married, set out once more and, leaving their vehicle at Westcott Farm (at the top of the Toll Road), fought their way on foot through the three and a half miles of snow which lay between them and the bulldozer. The last report the police received was that they had succeeded in reaching the machine and were in hopes of getting it started. Meanwhile they were staying with Lord Lytton and waiting for a helicopter to drop fuel supplies.'

If the people of the region were beginning to get to grips with the great blanket of snow which had smothered their New Year, their efforts were about to be frustrated. On Thursday 3 January, it snowed again so badly that a train on the West Somerset branch line – which had so far remained open – became stuck in drifts. Sixty soldiers from Doniford's army camp were brought in to extricate the 3.44 p.m. Taunton to Minehead train and, thanks to their sterling work, the service arrived at its destination just three hours late.

But things were far worse on the roads. Reports were coming in of some blockages being as high as 30 feet which prompted West Somerset and Exmoor highways surveyor Bill Donnan to comment: 'In terms of highway access our villages have been wiped out.'

The national press was beginning to take an interest and thanks to some entrepreneurial journalism by my father and photographer Randolph Priddy, the Brendon Hill doctor Maurice Hardman was about to hit the headlines. He was pictured skiing through deep snow in order to tend isolated patients and deliver medicines, but when I recently approached him on the subject he chuckled modestly: 'Never has anyone done so little to attract so much attention. If I recall I was only skiing down from my Leighland home to Prid the photographer's for the fun of the thing and a cup of tea. I suppose I may have had some medicine on me for one of the Roadwater villagers – but anyway, the story grew from there.'

One man who certainly needed medicine was farmer Bob Nancekivell at Cloud Farm, Oare, in the heart of Doone Country. He required insulin and to help the helicopter to find where to land his son Jim used coal dust to write the word 'CLOUD' in giant letters in the snow.

Another medical emergency – another helicopter. The *County Gazette* reported: 'Last Saturday, when fog closed down to add to the hazards, a helicopter crew made a mercy flight to carry a doctor to an injured youth on the Brendon Hills, and then conveyed him to Taunton.

'The day previously seventeen-year-old Sidney Payne of Lower Holworthy Farm, Kingsbrompton had been thrown from his horse and hurt his head. Overnight his condition deteriorated and, when he appeared to be much worse, Dr George Kelly, of Wiveliscombe, who was in telephone contact with his parents, appealed to the police for help.

'At that time a helicopter from Chivenor was standing on the recreation ground at Minehead where it had gone to pick up telephone engineers to fly them to Goosemoor, on the Brendons, for repair work. Because of foggy weather the helicopter was grounded and the flight called off. When the mercy call came through the crew of the helicopter took to the air without any hesitation, flying first to Wiveliscombe to pick up the doctor, and then out to the heart of the Brendons.

'They were absolutely marvellous,' farmer S. Payne told the reporter. 'I lit a beacon fire of straw and hoped they would see it through the fog. When I heard their engine I poured diesel oil on the fire and they came straight in. We have no words adequate to thank them.'

Fortunately the boy had suffered no serious injury and his only problem was how to get home through the snow from Taunton Hospital where he had been flown.

His father said: 'We are completely cut off by ten-foot drifts and can get no further than the farm gate. Luckily we had a good supply of food in and enough fodder for the animals so we are not going short.'

By 7 January the Ministry of Agriculture had realised the gravity of the situation and was organising a proper airdrop to remote farms on Exmoor and the Quantocks.

*The Bawden family of Hawkridge like most moorland farmers had to endure particularly difficult conditons in the winter of 1962/3.*
*Above: Taking in a rick of barley, 23 January.*
*Below: Hawkridge Post, 25 January.*

*The Ellerton Stores van breaks through to Hawkridge with much
needed supplies on 25 January. A week later the road was
completely blocked again by fresh snow.*

But the helicopters could not always get through because of fog and mist which regularly occurred in such conditions on the higher hills. When Mrs T.J. Hayes, of Withiel Florey on the Brendons, ran out of insulin a helicopter was despatched from Exeter but had to land short of its target at Brompton Regis. David Clayton of Dulverton then took over the delivery which he completed on skis.

It wasn't only drugs and hay bales which became airborne – shepherds and their sheepdogs also took to the skies in the trusty Wessex helicopters. Denzil Curtis (whose name has already been mentioned) and Russell Hicks were lifted out of Simonsbath to deal with flocks belonging to the Forstescue Estate, while Ernie Duke and his son Brian from remote Warren Farm a mile or two from that lonely village, were flown to nearby Kittucks where 200 Cheviot sheep were up to their necks in snow.

Villagers at Withypool were becoming concerned as their pantry shelves emptied. Even though a helicopter had managed to drop 18 loaves at nearby Landacre, something needed to be done to replenish the village's depleted larders and F.T. Barrow, D. Hawkins, Frank Blackmore, George Burnell, Keith Rich, David and Howard Pershouse, G. Barrow, Geoff Scoins and Len Morse decided to make a break for food with the help of the latter's racehorse. 'Royal Flame', as the horse was known, pulled their sledge through the snow to a rendezvous near Winsford with AA patrolman Robert Barrow who had escorted Dulverton baker Bern Balsom – and it was a proud gang of Arctic adventurers who returned home with a sledge laden with bread, milk and meat.

Indeed the central Exmoor villages acted like a chain of safe-houses for the delivery of many essentials which were hauled from one community to the next. For instance Exford postmen R.F. Cane, W. Saunders and G. Winzer had taken to walking towards Winsford to meet up with the mailbags which were being carried their way. Back at the village post office they sorted the mail and partly relied on a posse of volunteers to make many of the individual deliveries. They also dealt with the Simonsbath post which, at one time, accumulated to more than a hundredweight of parcels before it was collected by men who had made their way through ten foot drifts to collect it.

On one particular day, with a backlog of five days of mail to be delivered, R.F. Cane embarked upon a 20-mile round on foot through deep snow. It took him all day and at Horsen Farm he was told that he was the first person to call since Christmas.

As it had been for the likes of Harold Langsford in 1947, the delivery of mail took on a mantle of essential importance. Now, special mention was made of Albert Shopland whose Brendon Hill round took him far up into West Somerset snow away from his Alcombe home. Being born at Luxborough he knew the hills pretty well, but even he had difficulties in finding his way through the deep blanket. His round was taking him more than eleven hours to complete and often he had to rely on snowbound householders hearing his shout and coming out through the drifts to meet him.

Meanwhile Dick Lloyd, manager of the Honeymead Estate, had taken to delivering mail in his lonely neck of the woods on horseback.

By Saturday 12 January the *Somerset County Gazette* was reporting: 'For the first time in nearly a fortnight a trickle of traffic was able to negotiate the Williton to Taunton road on Thursday afternoon. It made for a spectacular drive for those who ventured upon it, with walls of snow higher than lorry cabs in places where bulldozers and excavators had cut through 12 foot drifts in the Crowcombe area.'

Only about half the area's schools were open – some closed because of burst pipes, but many were simply inaccessible to the children.

Taking stock as the communities began to grow accustomed to so much white stuff heaped upon the roof tops, letters and opinions on the big freeze were beginning to appear in the local newspapers. One came from hotel-keeper Holman of Simonsbath who commended the self-help attitude of his fellow villagers:

'Four times in the first fortnight a convoy of miscellaneous vehicles, in the charge of men of the village, fought their way across country in fearful weather, digging and winching those vehicles through and over drifts. They brought the village by far the largest part of its bread, milk, meat and fuel, and had a big part in distributing it to outlying farms. Thanks to this self-help, the whole of this scattered community has been provisioned.'

Over the hills to the north the Reverend Joseph Brunskill, Rector of Oare and Culbone, was also putting pen to paper. He called it the 'winter of the century' and described his Rectory as 'the end of the road' for the few supplies which found their way out to this remote spot. He and his wife had converted the Rectory pantry into a sort of parish store after a helicopter had landed with food supplies in the field opposite.

Between them and the outside world was the heavily drifted main road to Porlock which reporter Peter Hesp was able to describe having cadged a lift with County Council workmen:

'At the wheel Derek Cridland, of Washford, extolled the virtues of a four-wheel drive vehicle as we went slithering and roaring away up the second bend of that notorious hill (Porlock). I wish I could describe the sight which met us on top of the moor. The road as far as the AA Box was clear of really deep snow but all around for mile upon mile drifts rolled up like the phantom waves of some petrified sea. Up there not a single patch of ground or a bare twig or tuft of heather broke the unending white blanket. Although it was a fine day with no wind, the effects of a recent blizzard were strikingly apparent. Gorse-bushes and the stunted Exmoor trees had been transformed as if somebody had gone over every twig with a high powered spray-gun, coating everything with a layer of white plastic of such thickness that the whole coagulated into one mass.

'We stopped to have a word with two or three men who were endeavouring to dig out the road westwards from the AA Box. Their giant excavator and bulldozer looked like toys as they scrambled about in the piled up snow. A shepherd came by with a flock of Scottish Blackface sheep; I learned that while some flockmasters had got away without the loss of a single animal, others faced disaster. I was told that Mr J. Woolacott, a mile or two away in the Doone Country at Oare Ford, had lost 40 sheep which had died in drifts.

'We motored on – not along the road, which had completely disappeared, but over a rough track which had been cut across the open heath-land. It was a weird, desolate place, an expanse of even snow broken only by occasional mummified gorse-bushes looking for all the world like massive pieces of white coral. We might have been crossing some dead sea bottom. At Culbone Stables we rejoined the main road and met the excited men working on the big caterpillar.

'It was a ten minute walk from where they were working to the beginning of the big drift. Sheltered by the trees, the snow on the road was only a few inches deep; the air was calm and delightful, except for the crunching of snow underfoot there was a supreme silence broken at intervals by the alarming racket of a low-flying helicopter.

'We came to the end of the wood and stopped dead in our tracks. The open stretch of road ahead lay buried beneath a snow-drift. It was a frozen snow-drift and therefore we could climb it by kicking steps in its side like mountaineers. We climbed upwards for 15 or 20 feet and found ourselves on a plateau of snow which maintained its depth for as far as we could see. We discovered that this single drift of snow covered the road for nothing less than a mile-and-a-half.

'The crossbars of the telegraph poles were just clear of the snow. The telephone wires between the posts dipped down to touch the surface of the drift. Miraculously none of the wires seemed to have snapped, although each one had been transformed into an incredible garland of ice-flowers, hanging like a rope two inches thick.'

It was not really surprising that ice-flowers were growing on all that the freezing wind touched. A Fahrenheit reading of 22 degrees of frost was being recorded on Minehead's North Hill. Even the town's festive Christmas trees adorning the main streets stayed where they were, frozen

*Watchet Harbour frozen over in 1963.  First time in memory.*
*Jack Hurley on left.*  (K. Stockwell)

*A.39 West of Lillycombe, 1963.* (W.H. Donnan)

*Help by helicopter. Dulverton Station, 1963.* (V. Newton)

in place. The council workers were too busy dealing with the snow to worry about Twelfth Night.

A few miles away in Watchet things may have seemed colder still for two chilling reasons – one practical and one psychological. It was so cold that ice in the gasholders cracked a main, rendering the town's most important form of heating useless. And it was so cold that the harbour froze over pinning a big cargo boat to the wharf.

'The effect was a mass of disjointed ice like monster sugar cubes,' Jack Hurley observed of the scene in the harbour.

At Porlock water mains ceased to function and the normally fast-flowing Hawkcombe River froze. Here barometers were recording 30 degrees of frost.

As usual when such extreme conditions prevail, there were plenty of tales of valour and fortitude to keep the local press happy. One concerned twenty-three-year-old Thomas Priscott who was working on a farm near Wellington and became anxious for his elderly father Monro who farmed at Ash near Porlock, 800 feet above sea-level. Mr Priscott senior had only the help of another son, also called Monro, and – like many of their neigh-bours – they were having troubles with sheep being stuck in Exmoor's giant drifts.

There was only one thing for it as far as young Thomas was concerned – and that was a long and hazardous walk home. As the roads were blocked he took the cross-country route past Milverton and eventually to the main Taunton-Minehead road. As we've heard, this was fearsomely blocked in places, so Thomas had no choice but to walk on. In fact he was one of the first people to break through from the Taunton end of the route and he later reported that he was shown extraordinary kindness and hospitality along the way. He obviously couldn't have had much time to enjoy this hospitality: Thomas eventually reached Ash to help his brother with the sheep having walked some 40 miles in such extreme conditions!

There is a strange twist to this tale: Thomas Priscott's grandfather happened to be first cousin to the unfortunate Amos Cann whose death on a similar mission back in 1891 is reported in the early pages of this book.

A few miles from Ash, Nutscale Reservoir was being visited by Minehead's chief engineer K.G. Holman, who was flown there by RAF helicopter with chlorine gas for the chlorination plant. He found ice locked the surface of the reservoir to a depth of 11 inches.

Not far from Nutscale farmer R.W. Tucker of Lucott, Stoke Pero, was feeling miserable assuming that the worst had befallen a particular section of his flock he'd been unable to find. It was only when he noticed a number of starving foxes digging frantically at a drift that he was able to guess at the whereabouts of his missing stock. Sure enough there were the sheep deep under the snow – all alive and, after a good feed none the worse for their nine days spent inside a freezing drift!

Meanwhile a small army was at work on the county's blocked roads and by mid-January Somerset's road clearance bill had reached a then gigantic £250,000 with expenditure still running at £13,000 a day. Excavation plant had been brought in from as far afield as Leicestershire, and slowly but surely roads were being opened up all over the county and even on the hills.

## A Second Blast from the Freezer

Come early February the worst was generally believed to be over and there was every sign that a thaw might be in the air. But the great forces which had created this mini-ice-age had by no means finished with Southern England yet.

Tuesday 5 February was the thirty-eighth day of the snow siege of Somerset and by its afternoon people were beginning to realise there might well be more to come. By darkness a Force 9 gale blew from the south-east carrying with it a horizontal blizzard. In one night all the good work of the clearance teams disappeared under yet another white blanket.

As Bill Donnan put it: 'I have never seen anything like last night. It is impossible to distinguish fields from roads. We are worse off than we ever were.'

Because of this new wind direction drifts had occurred where no drifts were before. Exmoor had suffered a non-stop fall of thirty hours and surveyor Ron Rosser's Dulverton based men were out working in 'unbearable conditions' on the moorland roads – indeed 'conditions passed beyond endurance,' according to their boss who called them off the moor.

For the two road surveyors a massive headache was the problem of where to dump the snow which their machines would clear. All the available spots had been filled by piles dumped over that past month.

Back came the helicopters, much to the gratitude of some of the more remote communities. Parishioners in Withypool laid out a large Union Jack flag in a flat field near the village to guide in a Wessex which brought stocks of food. The big yellow helicopters were also used to fly snow-plough drivers out to their now stranded machines.

It was a wearisome journey which brought a 'whirlibird' (as they were affectionately known) to the aid of heavily pregnant Mrs Ann Dapling – and not a minute too soon. She lived out at remote Aclands Farm between Simonsbath and Challacombe and her worried husband Roger set off through the snow for help on Monday 11 February. First he waded to Driver Farm hoping to use the phone, but the lines were down. He was sent back to look after his wife while Mr G. Coward took over the baton on the race for help and struggled through the drifts to Simonsbath where he hoped to use the telephone at the Exmoor House Hotel. Alas this too was out of action, but at last he struck lucky at the Post Office from where P.C. Leonard Speed was contacted at Exford.

A helicopter carrying a doctor was arranged, but the women of the village, perhaps untrusting of such modern technology, set out for Aclands Farm to do whatever they could for the woman who was by now in labour. They needn't have worried – the trusty 'whirlibird' made an emergency dash across the snowy wastes, landed safely at the farm, and conveyed Mrs Dapling to a maternity home in Barnstaple where she gave birth to a baby son within little more than an hour of her arrival.

By the end of February Somerset's snow clearance bill had reached more than £525,000 and, as the work still continued through March, this figure climbed to over £650,000 – a massive slice of expenditure for a rural county. There was even some criticism of the way in which the job had been tackled, but the authority said in its defence, that no-one could have predicted such snow-fall and such low temperatures to occur for such a long period of time. Looking back over the years since the impartial observer would have to agree with this. More than 160 of the county's villages had been cut-off during the worst of the weather, some 350 blockages to roads had been caused by articulated lorries jack-knifing in the slippery conditions, and the normally well-stocked council had been forced to import salt from Spain, so much of the stuff had it used in its attempts to keep the highways open.

# 9  THE LAST BIG FALL
# OF THE CENTURY

The region has suffered many a snowfall since the Big One of '63 but none has come close to wreaking the havoc experienced by Westcountry folk during those three bitter months.

However, there was a week in late February of 1978 when those who could recall the 1963 freeze began to groan.  On Saturday 18 February the dreaded white stuff was falling thick and fast over the region.

Taunton librarian Elizabeth Searle was enjoying a white wedding with a difference.  Having only just managed to get through the blizzard to the church, her Westcountry honeymoon was a far more modest affair than planned. Instead of a wedding night spent at romantic Porlock Weir the happy couple had to make do with a stay at the Cross Keys Inn situated on the edge of Taunton.  It was as far as they could get.

That same night the less fortunate were in real danger of their lives, as the *Somerset County Gazette* reported:

'Two road workers, whose Land Rover was trapped by an avalanche at the height of the blizzard on the Brendon Hills, owe their lives to a cottage light which had been left on by mistake.

'Now safe in their Williton homes – although still suffering from frost-bitten fingers, Mr Len Routley and Mr Frank Rexworthy described their ordeal.

'As the blizzard grew worse on Saturday afternoon they had been sent out to recall a snow-plough driver near Treborough.  They never found him. The road disappeared under the drifts between Windwhistle and Coldharbour and they tried to turn back.

' " But when I began to reverse a great wall of snow collapsed into the road, burying us in an avalanche. We couldn't even open the doors to get out," said Mr Routley.

'Mr Rexworthy went on: "At first the engine heater kept us warm but soon we had to switch that off because of the fumes. The cold was terrible and as the snow sifted inside and began to fill the Land Rover, we started to shiver uncontrollably. Our clothes froze as hard as iron."

'The shrieking of the storm grew deafening and, in the early hours of Sunday morning, the men realised they were being buried alive.

' "Len wanted to stay but I kept remembering when I was a prisoner during the war and we were bombed inside cattle trucks. Suddenly I felt I had to get out. If we were going to die we would die outside,' said Mr Rexworthy.

'With a hammer they smashed a window and forced their way out. It was 4 am and they had been snowed in for nine hours. Soon they were utterly lost, although both were born and bred on the Brendons.

' "With the din and driving snow there was no sense of direction. It was difficult even to breathe and we had to crawl on our bellies, unable to stand. Nobody can know what it's like if they haven't been in such conditions. We both thought we'd had it," said Mr Routley.

'It was then that they saw the light. Mrs Fane Gladwin, who lives with her companion at Windwhistle Cottage, had let out her dog for a minute at bedtime and had forgotten to switch off the outside light. The men made for that light 250 yards away – and it took them nearly two hours to reach it.

' "They saved our lives," said Mr Routley. "They gave us bacon and eggs and stoked up the fire. It was marvellous."

'On Sunday the two men dug a way through to the garage where a food supply was stored in a freezer cabinet. They also dug out chickens and a pony.

'By teatime on Monday the two men were in Minehead Hospital, receiving treatment for exposure and frostbite, before being allowed home.'

In fact a number of travellers were caught out by the ferocity of the blizzard that night. On the Minehead – Taunton road drifts were piling up fast and local householders were finding themselves playing host to stranded motorists.

Barbara Henson, of Flaxpool Farm near Crowcombe, was dealing with a house-full of unexpected guests while her husband Jim was out doing the best he could for his stock.

'We found five ewes and nine lambs,' he was to tell the local press by phone on Monday. 'God knows where the rest are...'

Of her snowbound guests Mrs Henson said: 'One boy had set out to walk home from Taunton to Watchet. He had spent Saturday night at Cross Keys and reached us on Sunday night all in. Another couple had been more than seven hours walking from Williton and were in a state of collapse.'

Two other travellers to risk a chilly grave that Arctic night were Mr Phillip Main and Mr Mike Chilcott both of Williton, who had set out on Saturday night to collect the Sunday papers in Taunton.

Halfway at Red Post, near Triscombe – a section of the road always hard hit during a blizzard – the A 358 simply vanished into a deep drift in which both an ambulance and a snow-plough were already stuck.

'There was just nothing we could do and nowhere to go. It was impossible to turn back,' Mr Chilcott told reporters afterwards.

After a night spent shivering in their lorry the two men began a six-mile slog on foot back home – encountering 20-foot drifts on the way – staying with Mr Main's parents at Bicknoller on the Sunday night and eventually reaching Williton after a thirty-six-hour ordeal.

The *Somerset County Gazette* reported: 'On Wednesday all the vehicles which had been stranded at Red Post were still there, but their occupants had either walked out or taken refuge in local farms

'Miraculously there were no fatalities in the West Somerset area and police said everyone who had been reported missing was later accounted for.

'County council highways department teams worked day and night to clear emergency routes, although by midweek all roads into West Somerset were still blocked.'

So much for the combustion engine – now yesterday's technology was to come to the aid of the stranded district. Although the West Somerset Railway was under snow in many places and the diesel-electric locomotive found the going too tough, a solid piece of Victorian engineering was to come to the rescue in the form of steam engine which cleared its way through six-foot drifts!

The train provided valuable food drops for farms and communities along the track and by Wednesday it pressed on through to Bishops Lydeard to pick up mail for the stricken district behind the white hills.

In those hills farmers – and their beasts – were suffering.

Jim Henson told the *Gazette*: 'I've been here since 1928 and have seen nothing like it.'

In the heart of Exmoor on the Fortescue Estate at Simonsbath, dead sheep were dug out of the snow five deep, lacerated where they had fought to scramble out over each other's backs.

Typical of the plight of hill farmers was that of Mr John Pugsley, of Zeal Farm, Hawkridge. Surrounded by drifts as high as the house there was no way he could reach any of his stock.

'By now they must all be dead and there's nothing I can do,' he told reporter Peter Hesp. In places the snow had drifted to be more than thirty feet deep: no wonder that Hawkridge was cut-off for ten days and when finally relieved merited a mention in the national press.

Meanwhile, at Emmetts Grange Farm, near Simonsbath, Mrs A.R. Brown said the only way she could reach her ponies in their stable was to dig a tunnel under deep snow from her kitchen door!

A few airdrops were managed but by Monday a curtain of freezing fog shut out any chance of further aerial supplies.

And so, for a week, the region shivered its way through another mini ice-age – although this time the agony was to be short-lived. Within a week many of the area's roads were clear and, apart from a few flurries and freezes, the Westcountry had just about seen the last of twentieth Century snow.

# 10 A REGION OF FLOODS

We have already heard about the worst flood of them all when so many lives were lost in the 1952 tragedy at Lynmouth, but it would be wrong to complete a book on the region's stormy history without mentioning the regular deluges which have in the past made the lives of many a riverside dweller both uncomfortable and dangerous.

Today flooding is a far less common occurrence thanks to the many relief schemes which have been undertaken in the past 30 years – but even at the time of writing at the tail-end of the century, Exmoor and its surrounding areas still occasionally suffer the excesses of a flash-flood. And that is only to be expected in a location where high land abuts a gigantic ocean and takes the brunt of all too many of its water-laden weather systems. Indeed Exmoor has among the highest rainfall measurements anywhere in the south of England and, as anyone who has lived here for more than a year or two will know, heavy precipitation is common to say the least.

But, by and large our rivers rush and roar and our streams occasionally get too big for their boots without causing too much discomfort or damage as they hurtle down steep valleys on their way to the sea – valleys which now boast smooth concrete relief basins, in the old trouble spots, as well as works where rivers have been widened and straitened. Many old encumbrances and potential blockages have been removed so that those muddy brown waters can reach their destination without causing too much mayhem above and beyond the banks.

This wasn't always the case as, for example, any older resident from the village of aptly named Roadwater will tell you.

### *The Venice of Exmoor*

A far-fetched and fanciful appellation it may seem, but previous to the mid-1960s it was not at all uncommon to see men rowing down one stretch or another of Roadwater's long meandering main street. It really was a flood-village where locals grew angrily accustomed to heaving out the sandbags.

'Residents may send petition to Minister' stated a typical headline in the *Somerset County Gazette* in 1955. 'Feeling is running very high among the people of Roadwater since the bad flooding of 6 June ,' said the story referring to the fact that, despite promises to the contrary, the local council had done little to alleviate problem.

Said one local councillor, 'All that's been done is to send a man to Roadwater with a few drain rods.'

But it was going to take more than a few drain rods to sort out the problems of people like licensee Mrs I. Bailey and baker Mr C.O. Jago. Thanks to the flooding that week their very livelihoods were at stake. The Roadwater Inn was regularly isolated from the rest of the world – and potential customers – by floods while, just across the road, the bakery had been inundated to the extent that all of its supplies of flour where rendered unusable. And it wasn't just clean Brendon Hill water which swept through the village: the floodwaters brought with them 'the vilest stench'.

One rural district councillor shrugged his shoulders at the news: 'This is nothing new,' he said, 'the village has been more-or-less underwater for fifty years!'

Mind you, this particular freak summer storm had caused damage all over the area and so odd were the weather conditions that some Taunton residents reported seeing a thunderbolt crash through their gardens: 'It appeared to be vibrating as it came down and burst with a loud explosion when it hit the road, sending a shower of sparks up like a firework display,' said eyewitness Dorothy Carter, describing it as a red ball if fire which had hurtled down from the sky.

One elderly resident who remembers the flooding well is Mrs Queenie Taylor who was born just outside the village in 1910 and has lived there ever since. 'One of the worst I remember was back in 1931,' she told me.

*Roadwater – the Venice of Exmoor.* (Courtesy of John Nethercott.)

'We were living at Tacker Street by then and the water was a good three feet up the wall. I shall always remember that particular flood because we were meant to be having people over and my late husband Nobby went to Upton to get a couple of ducks for dinner. When he left the river was high, but when he came back he had a job to make it over to the house. The water came up so quickly.

'It washed the flowerpots from the window sills, that's how high it was,' recalls Mrs Taylor. 'But we were used to the floods and we knew what to do. You had to keep the water moving, that was the trick, and then the silt and mud wouldn't have time to settle in your home. When you thought it might flood you put what you could upstairs and the rest up on trestles.

'But I shall always remember that flood of 1931. Albert Burge came by and said he'd seen a drowned pig floating past. Of course The Valiant Soldier stayed open, even though the barrels were floating about around the bar! The men still went in for a drink in their Wellingtons.

'Further down in the village I remember Mrs Takle telling me how she'd come out of her cottage into the street when the flood had gone down, and tripped over a piece of furniture. "I wonder who that belongs to?" she thought to herself. But then she realised it was the top of her own side-board!

'I can also remember the pound notes from the Post Office being hung up to dry...'

Roadwater hit the newspapers once again in December 1960 when storm clouds gathered all over the Devon, Somerset and Exmoor areas to pour what they could onto already water-logged land.

But this time it was Porlock which dominated the headlines: 'A typical experience was that of Mrs M.E. Forty and her daughter Stella who have lived at Glen Cottage, Hawkcombe, Porlock, for the last fourteen years,' wrote Peter Hesp. 'They had laid out and cherished one of the most picturesque gardens in the locality. Holiday visitors used to come and take snaps on the little footbridge where a tiny stream threaded its way through the lawns and flowerbeds.

'When dawn broke on Sunday morning the two scared, tired women looked out of the window of their cottage and saw that the familiar scene had gone. All that remained of their garden was a few yards of path and ornamental wall near the house. Beyond was a roaring, foaming expanse of white water. The little footbridge had gone, of course; so had everything else – shrubs, lawn, soil, down to bedrock.'

'I can't believe it,' Mrs Forty told reporters. 'It was such a gentle little stream, a child could have paddled in it...'

Elsewhere in Porlock there were scenes of devastation, as there were in Bossington, Dunster, Washford, Roadwater, Exford and Williton.

It was a wet December. Bossington for instance, was flooded for a third time in a couple of weeks on Saturday 3rd – only to be inundated again on Tuesday.

Plans for flood relief works were speeded up after the December deluge, but people like Queenie Taylor remained unimpressed by the help local authorities offered to householders suffering flood-damage:

'They came around and said they would help us to redecorate. But we told them not to bother – they were only willing to paint up to where the flood-water had come, and no further.

'But they were bad floods, partly because no sooner had you got over one, then down came another.'

Fortunately, across Exmoor and its surrounding areas, the floods – and the blizzards – have been fewer and further between since the early 1960s, much to the relief of people living in the remoter, wilder and wetter parts of the Westcountry.

But you never know. Famous last words and all that.

In recent years I have heard many complain that winters are merging into summers, and vice-versa – and that the seasons aren't what they used to be. I know what they mean and far be it for me to lament the momentary lull in extreme weather which Mother Nature is most certainly capable of doling out in these parts.

But, whether wild meteorological conditions return or not, it is – just occasionally – an awesome and humbling experience to witness just how small and helpless we mere mortals are in the face of the great forces of Nature.

Despite all our advances in technology, if you are planning to spend more than the briefest of visits to the high moors in winter – well, you have been warned ...